PENGUIN
FAITH HE

Dr Rose is a clinical psychiatrist of wide experience who has worked in psychiatric hospitals and clinics with adults and children. During the war he commanded neurosis centres and psychiatric hospitals and was District Psychiatrist in North Africa and Italy. For twenty years he was a member of the Department of Psychological Medicine at St Bartholomew's Hospital, London, after which he was appointed the hospital's first Honorary Research Fellow in Psychological Medicine. He is a member of many associations and learned societies concerned with mental disability and its treatment, and has published papers on many of its aspects. Dr Rose has contributed to radio and television programmes. He has been actively interested in faith healing for many years.

# FAITH HEALING

## LOUIS ROSE

### EDITED BY BRYAN MORGAN

PENGUIN BOOKS

Penguin Books Ltd, Harmondsworth, Middlesex, England
Penguin Books Australia Ltd, Ringwood, Victoria, Australia

—

First published by Gollancz 1968
Published with revisions in Penguin Books 1971

—

Copyright © Louis Rose and Bryan Morgan, 1968, 1970

—

Made and printed in Great Britain
by C. Nicholls & Company Ltd
Set in Linotype Pilgrim

# Contents

Acknowledgements      8
Foreword by Dr D. J. West      9
Introduction      11

## PART ONE

1. Priest and Physician      23
2. From the Stroker to the Magnetist      41
3. Latter-Day Healers      60
4. In the Eyes of the Church      87
5. Many Questions, Some Answers      111

## PART TWO

6. Investigation      141

Conclusion      175
Postscript by Professor
W. Lindford Rees      178
Works Consulted      180
Index      184

# Acknowledgements

I AM indebted to my collaborator Bryan Morgan for examining and collating my material and in particular for his considerable help in planning and editing this book.

In the days of attending meetings and discussions and following up inquiries my wife, with great patience, collected the notes and records for filing and cross-referencing: I owe her much. Help and occasional prodding with news of fresh 'miracles' have derived from Mrs K. M. Goldney, one of the vice-presidents of the Society for Psychical Research. Other various and varied personal communications have, I think, added colour and breadth to my inquiry: among those who have helped are Professor H. H. Price of Oxford, Professor H. Bender of Freiburg, Professor H. Urban of Innsbruck, Mr W. Roll of Duke University, Dr Griffith Edwards of the Maudsley Hospital and Dr D. Bannister of Dartford Hospital, Bexley, Kent.

Although he is mentioned throughout the book Mr Harry Edwards must be accorded specific acknowledgement. I do not deny his good faith, and though we meet rarely it is on friendly terms even though we continue to disagree on paper.

Finally, I must say how much I appreciate the speedy and efficient preparation of drafts and revised versions by my secretary, Mrs Isabel Vincent. She has also been most helpful with research and in particular with checking suspected errors in the first edition of this book. This has contributed greatly to what I hope will now be a definitive text. Both Mr Morgan and I are most grateful for her devotion to this task.

# Foreword

BY D. J. WEST

*Assistant director of research, Institute of Criminology.*
*Sometime research officer to the Society for Psychical Research.*

UNEXPLAINED faith cures, because they are more difficult to investigate than some of the simpler claims of clair-
voyants, have been undeservedly neglected by students of
the paranormal. Now Dr Louis Rose, a medical man of
sober judgement and one admirably qualified to pursue
this topic, has made a start. It must have taken considerable determination, for the subject is fraught with ham-
pering emotional commitments to an even greater extent
than the still controversial question of the existence of
telepathy. On the one hand, some established religions are
committed to belief in miraculous cures; and many
modern healers and their followers, both secular and religious, proclaim that cures which baffle medical science
are everyday occurrences. On the other hand, medical
guardians of the status quo see no justification for taking
these claims seriously, no reason to test the matter by letting paranormal healers try to help their patients under
supervision, and no cause to allow students access to the
medical records of persons said to have been cured miraculously.

The matter is complicated still further by the ambiguity
of the concept of paranormal cure. Successful divination
of the order of a set of cards in a sealed envelope calls for
a clear-cut decision between the paranormal and the
fraudulent, but a successful cure of asthma or epilepsy, for
example, gives rise to a more complicated array of differ-

ent interpretations. The limits of the possible and the normal in regard to the effects of suggestion and auto suggestion, to say nothing of the unaided powers of spontaneous recuperation, are far less well-defined than is popularly supposed. Changes that would be self-evidently paranormal, like the regeneration of a lost finger, do not arise in the context of modern faith healing.

Like all investigators who have taken the trouble to follow up the testimony of witnesses to extraordinary events (whether concerned with seance room phenomena, flying saucers, radiaesthesia, prophesies or miracle cures), Dr Rose has had the experience of lengthy battles against reluctance and obstruction ending with the discovery that what had seemed promising evidence at first sight generally turned out to be extremely dubious or exaggerated. The crucial issue, however – the importance of which can hardly be over-estimated – is whether a residuum of established fact exists. In producing this book Dr Rose has made one of the first tangible contributions towards finding the answer.

D.J.W.

# Introduction

THE legend runs that about the year AD 615 a young Welsh girl named Winefride was pursued by her lover Prince Caradoc on her way to church. Determined as she was to become a nun she resisted his advances, which piqued the prince so much that he chopped off her head at the church door. But fortunately the priest there was St Beuno who, as well as being the girl's uncle, was a considerable worker of miracles. The thaumaturge picked up Winefride's head and replaced it in position, where it grew again leaving (according to the chronicler, Robert of Shrewsbury) only a slight scar.

Incidents such as this can be found in the mythology if not the official hagiography of many saints, and are manifestly examples of 'paranormal' activity. But as a student I learned that in the opinion of many physicians as good a way as any of banishing a wart was to make a mysterious sign over it with a piece of potato and mutter something, preferably in Latin. These two examples – the one of an alleged single event, the other of a technique almost as frequently employed as are aspirin tablets – may be of limited historic and scientific value. But they will serve to typify two extremes in a whole class of phenomena which is commonly labelled 'faith healing'.

The term is thoroughly unsatisfactory, being so ambiguous that it is not even clear whether the faith which may or may not be responsible for certain therapeutic processes (which themselves may or may not take place) is a quality of the healer or the healed. I do not always see eye to eye with Mr Beverley Nichols, but I found myself in sympathy with him recently when he compared the present 'state of the art' of effecting cures by means other than those of orthodox medicine to the position of the Christian church in the apostolic age. Both had many enthusiasts, many puzzled and half-convinced observers, many marvels or rumours of marvels; but neither could call upon a central, established basis of fact or belief and there was not even an agreed terminology. Virtually every writer on this subject has indeed been struck by the vast verbal confusion at its very root, a confusion which has also befogged the work of such committees and councils as have attempted to come to grips with it.

For example, in *The Church's Ministry of Healing*, published some twelve years ago, the Archbishops' Commission commented that the term 'faith healing ... is far from precise and may imply that a prerequisite of healing is belief in the healer's powers, or belief that the sufferer will, in fact, recover, or belief that God wills recovery from the particular ailment'. They went on to say that the phrase 'spiritual healing ... is one which is used by certain healers who claim to be agents of doctors in the "spirit world"; it may, therefore, easily be misunderstood. This in itself is not a good reason for discarding it; but there is a more serious objection. By appropriating the word "spiritual" to certain methods of healing it implies that other methods are necessarily not spiritual.' Finally, with regard to 'divine healing', they stated 'The term could ... be taken to imply that those who have some special gift of healing and who work outside the Church's life and fellowship have not received their gift from God.'

Most workers in the field take particular exception to the term 'faith healing', but it does have one important virtue: for most of us it immediately brings to mind the range of phenomena which forms the subject of this book. We may, for convenience, describe such phenomena as those in which physical illnesses appear to be cured by means other than those of drugs, surgery, regimes, manipulations, recognized psychological methods or common sense, but which are not included in another group which includes acupuncture – the techniques of which, controversial though they may be, are at least teachable and largely independent of the personality of the practitioner. 'Paranormal' healing might be a better term, but it is somewhat clumsy and perhaps begs the question.

I think, therefore, that it will be for the best if we allow ourselves the occasional use of the familiar phrase 'faith healing' so long as it is understood that its use does not imply the acceptance of any particular philosophy of the subject. It should, however, be noted here that even those whom the public regard as leading exponents of faith healing are often themselves opposed to the use of the phrase and prefer such descriptions as 'spirit healing', 'spiritual healing' or 'divine healing'. The religious, however, regard *all* therapy as divine; and many of all persuasions regard the simple term 'healing' as sufficient identification.

Such, then, is the subject of this book. It is not an esoteric subject nowadays, for several new publications on it appear in Britain alone each year and a select bibliography already fills a sizeable pamphlet. Indeed, there has in recent years been a remarkable upsurge of public interest in all forms of 'fringe' medicine – an upsurge which may be explained, according to individual taste, as a healthy reaction against establishments (and particularly against the combination of surgery, allopathic medication and immunization which has dominated medicine since the Renaissance), a protest against the mechanistic and a return to the tradition of regarding man as a complex of the physical and the spiritual, a rediscovery of old wisdom, a demand for marvels or simply a relapse into superstition and quackery.

But by far the greater part of this literature, even of that written with moderation and containing a proportion of historical and scientific objectivity, consists of the works of the committed – of convinced Spiritualists, Roman Catholics, 'Christian Scientists', Methodists or those who bear no particular banner but are simply convinced of the efficacy of paranormal healing. A much smaller contribution has come from those who are equally – and sometimes less frankly and on less evidence – committed to disbelief. Some of these latter have perhaps looked more sceptically at Christian miracles than at the cures claimed by Spiritualists.

Since I have tried to make my own standpoint one of complete objectivity, this book contains nothing for those seeking 'inspirational' literature, for proof that no disease is incurable, for easy comfort. Nor is it a history of miracles. Certain 'cures' are reported at their face value for the sake of simplicity, since it is not necessary for me to carry the burden of the crime journalist who must constantly include in his text such words as 'alleged' and 'claimed'. But the absence of these reminders does not mean that such cures can necessarily be accepted as verified.

In one respect, however, I am in full agreement with the uncritical adherents of faith healing: I believe this to be a phenomenon important and common enough to call for serious study. If it takes place (and there is evidence that *something* beneficial happens to *some* sufferers) then it should be brought into line with the main body of medical knowledge; for, regardless of the immense scientific, philosophical and spiritual implications and considering economic factors alone, a validated faith-healing service could mean the saving of millions of pounds yearly on drugs and hospitalization in Britain alone. If it does *not* work (and the evidence on this side, like most negative evidence, is much less colourful), then the efforts of the faith healers are at best a waste of time and at worst a conscious or unconscious deception which might influence sufferers to neglect orthodox medical treatment.

Over eighteen years ago I became so engrossed in this subject that I decided to devote as much time as I could spare to elucidating this question: are the claims of the faith healers, and their proportion of successes, based on more than the operation of the laws of chance and techniques of persuasion and suggestion? To make headway across this immense and misty field lying between science and religion would obviously be difficult. But it should prove a rewarding challenge, since there were few disinterested investigators working on the subject.

Before proceeding, I should perhaps explain my original attitude. I was in no way setting myself up as a ghost-hunter; on the contrary, I started my quest in the hope that it would lead to a validation of the view of the majority (which, according to one survey, forms over four fifths of the population of Britain) holding that there is 'something behind it all', even if I did not join the estimated one million subscribers to the National Health Service who prefer the ministrations of unorthodox healers. If this is not a book of wonders, neither is it an exposé based on any antipathy.

What, then, is it? As my interest in the subject became more generally known I was frequently asked what I was trying to prove, so I feel that I should make my position clear. I was trying to prove nothing and disprove nothing. My aim was only to work on a project which interested me and if possible discover the truth. Even if I doubted whether I would make any real progress, I had the hope of adding to my own knowledge and experience and, if I was fortunate, of making a contribution that would prove useful to others as well.

In essence, then, this book is the record of a search for truth, a truth which I have tried to establish through two main channels which correspond to its two sections. The first of these is the documentary or historic approach; and here, while undertaking little primary research, I have tried to bring together a mass of data on the claims of paranormal healers hitherto scattered amongst many books. Then, after an attempt to analyse and co-ordinate this material, I have moved on to a presentation of the results of my own inquiries into the subject, which have been conducted from the standpoint of a clinical psychiatrist. Some of this latter material has already appeared, in a different form, in medical and other specialized journals.

Early on I recognized a moral question : if the facts eventually at my disposal refuted the *objective* claims of faith healers, then there was a danger that sufferers who were gaining *subjective* benefit from such treatment might lose confidence in it – and I have never believed in depriving patients of any regime which they believed to be beneficial unless it was manifestly harmful. I consulted a number of thoughtful men, including priests and philosophers, on this matter, and was glad to find them virtually unanimous in agreeing that whatever I could contribute concerning the truth about faith healing was a matter of public concern and should be made available to any interested person.

It was clear, even so, that both my investigations and my reporting on them would be accompanied by considerable difficulties. I therefore felt it necessary to avoid sidetracks as far as possible : and perhaps the most seductive of these by-ways was the likelihood of becoming involved in asking too many questions concerning the mechanism of faith cures. At first I did indeed ponder this aspect of the problem; but I soon realized that there was no point in exploring mechanisms until the basic facts were clear. (As an instance of this distinction, I may quote the example of an international conference on healing which I attended. When our chairman announced that the aim of the meeting was to try to reach some agreement on *how* faith cures took place, I countered with the suggestion that the first problem was surely to determine whether in fact such cures *did* take place. The conference was perhaps never the same afterwards: certainly my relations with its sponsors were not.) Thus, should we find that – for instance – prayer at a certain shrine led to fifty per cent of cures which could not reasonably be challenged, it would be no major matter for us to ask why an equal number of prayers went unanswered. To substantiate the claim itself would be enough of an undertaking.

Further, our first concern is with physical rather than mental states and we need hence not become involved with – for instance – theories of diabolical possession or techniques of control over pain. 'Fringe' medicine in general – particularly when its methods have psychic overtones – is another subject only marginal to our present one, as I discovered when I became diverted from the main line of my investigation into a study of radiaesthesia. Needless to say, one is also frequently brought up against beguiling problems of semantics and of the philosophy and methodology of science. And two other fields which can receive little more than a mention in this introductory note are the state of paranormal research generally and the proper relation between faith healers and the orthodox medical profession.

On the first score we must recognize that, despite such statements as Professor Eysenck's that 'the only conclusion that the unbiased observer can come to must be that there does exist a small number of people who obtain knowledge ... by means as yet unknown to science', the question of the 'ESP' or 'psi' faculties persistently remains an open one. On the one hand one sees even palmistry being taken seriously for diagnostic purposes in the USA: on the other, there remains a hard core of materialists as prejudiced against all such concepts as were their grandfathers against the concept of microbes. Were the truth about telepathy, precognitive dreams and the like known, then perhaps more light would be thrown on the activities of faith healers, for a part of their art would appear to involve the faculty (which was seriously debated by Jung) for psychic diagnosis or 'telegnosis'. But it would be only a *little* more light, and the central problems of faith healing would remain.

A not-unrelated consideration, though one which seems to be generally overlooked by the adherents of psychic healing, is that just as a lively faith in God leads to a corresponding one in the Devil so would a valid 'white magic' of faith healing lead to credence in the black magic of harming and killing one's enemies. But here again I have had firmly to avoid the temptation to explore an enticing sidetrack.

As to the second consideration mentioned above, one need say little more than that faith healers of all persuasions have won the right to practise openly in Britain (as they cannot in most of the Germanic countries) and are allowed to visit hospitals – though they are not yet awarded the courtesy title 'doctor' as they are in Canada. But if we take a perspective view of the development of medicine, both as a body of thought and a profession, it may be possible to see why some practitioners still feel threatened by such phenomena as faith healing, hypnosis and the idea of mind-body interaction generally. A study of its history suggests that in the early times when medicine was bound up with religious ideas there was nothing to prevent the physician considering his patient as a whole person. The eighteenth and nineteenth centuries, however, saw the rapid advance of the physical sciences and the incorporation into medicine of demonstrable facts concerning physiology generally and the pathology of disease in particular.

The effect of this knowledge was enormous, since it transformed the physician from a man nearly helpless in the face of sickness into a member of an army very much on the march. However, it carried with it certain assumptions.

These were not generally worked out or set down on paper because medical men, then as now, were as a body involved in the practical demands of their patients and not greatly inclined to concern themselves with the philosophical implications of their profession. But they remain important.

The main assumption underlying the early medicine of the modern era was a simple dualism which argued that body and mind were utterly separate and that the physician could safely attend to the one and leave the other out of account. Fortunately for their patients, the common sense and personal experience of practitioners made them, in their work, much more aware of the importance of psychological factors than the orthodox official position implied. But it is only some fifty years since the term 'shell shock' was invented by those who would not recognize the possibility that a combat environment might in itself produce physical effects, and many medical men still seem to feel that the purity of physical medicine is threatened by psychiatric interference. Their resentment is naturally all the greater when such intervention comes from the medically unqualified; and it may well be that this hostility has driven many faith healers and kindred spirits into a more extreme position than they would otherwise have taken.

A final simplification is enforced by the fact that it is difficult to treat the historical aspects of this subject from what has come to be called a 'global' viewpoint. I recognize that I am a western man writing primarily *for* western men whose thoughts are inevitably coloured by the Greco-Roman-Judaic traditions of Europe and (to a lesser degree) of North Africa and the closer regions of Asia. There may be light to be thrown on the phenomena of paranormal healing by the experience of the civilizations of the Far East and of primitive tribes – or, for that matter, of the Greek Orthodox church or the rabbinical healers who were influential in Tolstoy's Russia. But though I have been tempted into discussions of yoga, the influence of the caste system on Indian medicine and the like, I have generally recognized these too as sidetracks. My colleagues working in primitive Africa have developed the thesis that the psychiatric illnesses of their patients belong in a quite different spectrum from those of western man; and in any case it appears that the experience of exotic civilizations does little more than expand without illuminating the body of material available nearer at hand. This body is so considerable that when dealing with modern times I have had to concentrate experience still further and draw mainly on British material.

Plato complained that it was the greatest error of his day that in medical treatment physicians separated the concept of the soul from that of the body. Much more recently, Dr Cyril Burt stressed that physicians should not look upon a patient as 'a potential corpse to which a ghost is loosely attached' and Professor Ryle used the phrase 'the ghost in the machine'. Psychology has already done much to round out the concept of man which medicine can – and must – reasonably accept. But is the evidence for some form of paranormal intervention in human sickness so strong that, in addition to considering the complex interactions of mind and body, therapy must take account of yet another element called the soul?

The Rev. Bertram E. Woods, one of the more thoughtful of the religiously-committed students of this subject and one who acknowledges its complexity, recently wrote, 'It is time an investigation was made into the whole field of spiritual healing. There never was a time when so much material was available to the researcher.' This book is an attempt to do something to organize as well as to add to that material, even if the full investigation which the subject demands must still be left to the future.

# PART ONE

CHAPTER ONE

# Priest and Physician

MAN has always looked to religion to fulfil two basic needs. Firstly, the world must make sense to him; and, secondly, he must feel himself to be more than the slave of implacable fates, gods or mechanistic laws.

From the earliest civilizations – and often before ideas of morality or immortality became involved – priests, elders of the tribe and witch doctors recognized these dual needs and attempted to satisfy them. On the one hand they were expected to *predict*, for example, that the dark days would lengthen and the river refill its banks. On the other, their prestige was increased by signs that they could also *control* natural forces by prayer and incantation.

This control, when a knowledge of natural forces which they were careful to keep secret became adequate to enable them to predict comets and eclipses, they certainly *seemed* to exercise. It is hence not surprising that the still more vital human tasks of determining the causes of illness and of prescribing cures for it should pass to those who could apparently both explain and influence the behaviour of the powers believed to rule the world. As an Egyptian papyrus reads, 'He who treats the sick must be expert in magic, learned in the proper incantations and know how to make amulets to control disease.'

Today our priests mainly perform more human and humble offices, and only in the Mass is it the duty of the priest to take part in a routine, if invisible, miracle: the prediction of natural events has become the task of the scientist. But one form of physical behaviour still refuses to be classed with the exact sciences. It is that associated with the diagnosis, prognosis and cure of human ailments.

Even today, then, medicine retains a certain aura of mystery. But in early civilizations priest and physician were one, though the study of surviving 'Stone-Age' cultures suggests that even before the age of written records a division was drawn between religion – the formal observances of the tribe – and the magical procedures which were directed to the healing of individuals. For instance, in the middle-eastern cultures of about 3000 BC the standard method of treating disease was the casting out by incantation of the malevolent spirit believed to be causing it. There was often also a recommendation to follow a herbal diet, and 'sympathetic' rites which might involve water and incense were practised too. Prognosis was guided by divination from the stars and animal remains.

Certain herbs appeared to have intrinsic merit, though it was hard to determine how great this was since their administration was in any case accompanied by magical rites and their successes glossed by religious exegeses; and together with a surgery of uneven sophistication and greater attention to nursing these added to the therapeutic armament of the Greek and Roman world. But even when men began to doubt the intervention of the gods in human affairs generally they were reluctant to deny it in medicine. The classical physician might privately believe his art to be the empirical one of prescribing what had been prescribed before and found to be effective; but his patient would probably expect the name of Aesculapius – the son of Apollo and father of Hygeia who was nevertheless only a Grecian avatar of Imhotep, the Egyptian demi-god of healing – to be invoked as well. If the treatment was successful it was probably honoured by such votive plaques as adorned the splendid temples of Epidaurus: this tradition too was inherited from the Egyptians (who believed that anything left behind by a patient who had been cured itself had prophylactic powers), and of course remains common today in Roman Catholic churches.

Similarly, the classic civilizations adopted the practice of the 'incubation temples' in which sufferers passed a night (for instance, in the tomb of Imhotep) in the belief that the gods would cure them in a dream. So popular – and apparently successful – were these that they were frequently the last centres of paganism to hold out against Christianity, and indeed the practice itself entered Christendom. In the Middle Ages, for instance, churches were sometimes equipped with mattresses and even baths for this purpose, a church in Cambridge being particularly renowned for its incubation cures: and the practice is not yet extinct in the Greek Orthodox persuasion and in certain corners of Roman Catholicism.

Nor did the practitioner himself (who was often fully aware of the psychological element in healing, of the importance of the patient's faith in his physician and in the treatment he was receiving) always discount the efficacy of supernatural elements. About 450 BC Empedocles, though a pioneer of scientific medicine, seems to have been willing to be regarded as a magic-making priest too, and Galen wrote about AD 180, when considering the more primitive beliefs of his age, that 'some think they are like old wives' tales, as I too did for a long time. But at last I was convinced that there is virtue in them by plain proofs before my eyes'. Elsewhere (and with some insight) Galen seems to suggest that the virtues of the healing temples were not intrinsic but due to some form of mental mechanism. But outside the stream of early rational medicine there was a widespread popular credence in the general powers of miracle-working wizards like Serapis and Apollonius of Tyana, as well as such specific beliefs as that to sleep with the fourth book of the Iliad below one's pillow would produce a cure for quartan ague.

Beyond the Greco-Roman world, belief in healing magic was yet more common. For instance, the Persians recognized three forms of physician whose respective tools were the knife, the drug and the spell, and considered the last the best: in the Far East therapy had to take into account the work of gods, demons and ill-wishers: and in the Judaic scriptures paranormal cures such as the answer to Abraham's prayer against barrenness and those of leprosy by Moses and Elisha take their place beside miracles of prediction.

The Old Testament prophets, though, were primarily interested in more general matters of social hygiene, and they are credited less with individual cures than with restoring the dead to life and prophylactic measures such as Moses' protection of the Jews from snake-bite. At times an element of fatalism was evident in this culture; but though the Jews believed that disease would not be banished until the Messiah came they were not generally hostile to orthodox medicine and most of the thirty-eighth chapter of Ecclesiasticus indeed forms a hymn to the art of the few physicians of the Preacher's time. A special case was that of Solomon, the all-powerful 'white' magician whose reputed talents included the gifts of paranormal healing.

Turning to the great figures of the Indic culture of the East from 1000 to 100 BC – to the Buddha and Krishna, for instance – we again meet claims for magical cures appearing side by side with herbal remedies. In general though – and despite the equation of the *prana* or life force of yoga with some form of healing power – the tradition here is one of withdrawal from, rather than intervention in, the visible world, with the eastern belief in reincarnation providing a further complicating factor: it was considered, for example, that a likely cause of toothache was that one had drunk too much alcohol in a previous existence. In any case, for western man the outstanding figure now becomes that of Jesus of Nazareth, if only because it has been estimated that one verse in every seven of the Gospels, and one in fourteen of the Acts, refers to the type of therapeutic activity which convinced John the Baptist that this was more than another magus on the fringe of the Judaic and Greco-Roman traditions representing a cult such as that of the Essene healer-priests, and was indeed *the* Christ.

Some fifty paranormal events are ascribed to Christ in the four Gospels. (It is perhaps worth noticing here that one of the evangelists was himself a physician, and that no word of Christ's can reasonably be interpreted as hostile to the physical medicine of His time.) Less than three dozen of these 'miracles', though, can be classed as healings if resurrection from the dead is excluded, and of these many were at the time recognized as referring to psychological states and explained as being exorcisms of evil spirits. Perhaps half the remainder concern *possible* psychiatric disorders.

Cures of organic disease are, however, recorded in Mark v of a haemorrhage or 'issue of blood' which was healed without Christ's will, in Luke xiv of dropsy, in Mark iii of a withered hand and in Matthew viii and elsewhere of fevers: in the first case the commentator tells us that the female patient 'had suffered many things of many physicians, and spent all that she had, and was nothing bettered, but rather grew worse'. At least four cures of blindness are recorded, and in addition two works attributed to Christ are of special interest.

One of these is the healing of a centurion's servant, mentioned in Matthew viii, which appears to be the first recorded claim of a paranormal cure in which the sufferer did not know that he was being treated. The other (Luke xxii) is the treatment of the Jewish servant of the high priest, Malchus, after St Peter had impulsively sliced off his ear on the night before the Crucifixion. This is the only example in the Gospels of a detached member being replaced, and its authenticity is doubted by some biblical scholars.

Christ's techniques included prayers and commands to be well, the laying on of hands, and instructions to the sufferer to pursue a certain course of action: there is some evidence that the simpler methods were used for mental illnesses. The faith of the patient seems sometimes to have been important, and in one case (described in Luke viii) that of witnesses too. Christ also appears to have presided over ten 'mass' healings – for example, that recorded in Luke iv – and according to one claim *all* who touched Him were made whole.

After His death legends grew up around the figure of the Saviour. One, for instance, states that He cured St Peter of toothache, whilst the Greeks identified Him with Aesculapius. But at the same time the pattern of Christ's cures was continued by His disciples, who formed an early church in which salvation was understood to include physical, mental and spiritual health, where sickness was barely distinguishable from sin, and where the word 'therapy' bore its original significance of 'service'. These disciples were charged to heal in five separate dicta of Christ's, most of which implied that their faith was the source of their special powers. Typical orders were 'Heal the sick, cleanse the lepers, raise the dead, cast out devils' (Matthew x). In Mark xvi they received the promise that they should 'lay hands on the sick; and they shall recover'.

There are no accounts of apostolic 'absent' cures, however, and in general these later healings appear to have a higher content of suggestion than do Christ's own. There is even some evidence that, after the descent of the Holy

Ghost at Pentecost had first inspired St Peter to a healing act, the therapeutic powers of the early Christians showed a slow but steady decline as they became more remote in time and spirit from their Founder. From 1 Corinthians, however, it appears that many of the earlier priests were selected for their gifts of healing.

Concerning the successes, we read, in addition to accounts of exorcisms, that St Peter and St John cured a lame man from Solomon's porch at the Beautiful Gate of Jerusalem. For this they were arrested but later released, and shortly afterwards the apostles held a 'mass' healing service at the same place. Four other followers of Christ – St Stephen, St Philip, St Barnabas and St Paul – also conducted group meetings. Paul himself, who seems to have lost his sight in the shock of conversion, had it restored by Ananias, and there were apostolic individual healings of snake-bite, blindness and dysentery.

The methods employed included laying on of hands and verbal commands, and of St Peter it was said that even his shadow restored health (Acts v). Objects touched by St Paul were also believed to cure disease, but this apostle certainly did not rely on faith alone and advised Timothy to drink more wine. He omitted to heal Trophimus, and in 1 Corinthians suggested that healing was a charismatic or personal gift.

On the whole, though, the record of paranormal healing in early Christian times was so impressive that the methods of the disciples were copied – apparently with some success – by unbelievers (Acts xix). At this period of Roman culture physicians were few and their services costly: indeed, theologians consider that one of the reasons for the growth of the early Christian church was its concern for the sick (and hence sinful) who were otherwise despised.

In the next age of Christianity, that of the fathers of the

church of the second, third and later centuries, sufferers continued to be treated on a large scale: failure to heal was indeed regarded by some as evidence of sin on the part of the healer. In particular, Hermas wrote that it was a 'great joy' to free men from suffering, Tatian asked why men should use herbs when God could heal everything, the great Origen stated that a faith in Christ was more effective than one in Aesculapius, Irenaeus said that true believers – and *only* true believers – could cure many diseases, cast out devils and even raise the dead (as he claimed to have witnessed in rare cases), Tertullian, Justin Martyr, Ambrose of Milan and Quadratus also spoke of the importance of spiritual healing, Gregory Thaumaturgus was held to work the miracles which his name suggests, and healing saints – who often ministered to beasts as well as men – included St Aphraates, St Genovefa and St Hilarion. From the other side, Julian the Apostate despised Christians for their habit of consorting with the diseased.

In the fourth century, however, St Chrysostom remarked that though healing still took place miracles were becoming rare. The tradition certainly endured into the age of St Augustine, who claimed to have witnessed therapeutic and other wonders and who himself is reported, in an account which runs to more than three pages, to have prayed with another bishop for a Carthaginian civil servant called Innocent who had a fistula covering his entire body: after this, the lesion vanished overnight. But already leading figures such as Fabiola were founding hospitals rather than attempting spiritual cures, and the latter were becoming the province of Alexandrian mystical sects such as the gnostics and neoplatonists.

Furthermore, though a prayer for healing powers was still included in the rites of ordaining a priest, a belief was spreading which was to become increasingly important in Catholic Christian theology – though not exclusive to it, for it dates back at least to the time of Elisha. This was that cures could be obtained, not only through the offices of living healers but also through the relics (or at the shrines) of those who had led especially saintly lives or had been martyred for their faith. Many such persons, indeed, came to be credited with healing acts after their death even when there was no record of their having been responsible for cures while they were living.

From Martin of Tours in the fourth century to John of Beverley in the seventh, paranormal cures were still being reported at the hands of the living. But after the conversion of Constantine and his empire to Christianity, and then the Council of Nicaea, the philosophy of the church changed as it began to exert a dominance over western thought which was to endure for more than a thousand years.

It became more formalized, with matters of definition and organization assuming first importance and intellectual qualities taking precedence over spiritual talents. It looked to the practices of its past rather than to the gifts of its living members, and its rites directed greater attention to Christ's instructions to remember His last supper than to His injunction to work (or attempt to work) other miracles in His name: so far as therapy was concerned, this attitude was perhaps encouraged by the improvements in physical treatment which Greek influence brought to the later Roman Empire. Revelation was considered complete, and there was hence a certain return to the fatalism of the old covenant which regarded all phenomena, including disease, as immediate expressions of God's will.

This will might be modified by prayer, though it was better to bear pain patiently and to concentrate on perfecting the soul: direct action was considered impious. The tradition of paranormal healing was half-forgotten, and even physical cures came into disrepute in an age when men were taught to regard belief in Christ as the complete solution to all human problems. As early as AD 360, for instance, a bishop was condemning physicians as magicians; and two centuries later the emperor Justinian attempted to close the medical schools in his province.

Even the monastery hospitals of the Dark and early Middle Ages, such as those (as at St Albans) which were founded in a revival of medicine about AD 800 or the later establishments of such orders as the Knights Templar, generally concentrated more on providing infirmaries to prepare for a godly death than on true therapy. The situation degenerated since priests were believed to add to their income by selling cures (a scandal which led to condemnation by the Lateran Council of 1123): surgery was forbidden the religious since it involved the shedding of blood: and there were genuine misunderstandings of papal edicts. Hence, though individual healing saints continued to practise their art, most such attempts at paranormal healing as took place in the western church did so within two strictly-prescribed formulae.

These were the sacrament of unction – the anointing of the dying with holy oil, perhaps taken from the lamp on a saint's tomb, which was based on a verse in James v and may have begun as a physical cure – and the exorcisms regularized by the Council of Antioch in 341. Nor, despite an upsurge of interest in physical healing in their culture around the twelfth century, did the Jews of the later Rabbinical period develop as much interest as had their forebears in medical treatment. Paradoxically, it was at this period left to the more confessedly fatalistic followers of Mahommet not only to make progress in orthodox medicine but to produce the saints of 'miracle' healing too.

But western Europe did not go entirely without attention. If neither priest nor physician could offer help then the village leech, barber, apothecary, witch or wise woman could; and despite the occult powers attributed to those in special situations (such as the seventh sons of seventh sons), and the Celtic legends of great healing wizards such as Merlin and Taliesin, it was these who provided most of the therapy of medieval Britain.

The methods and apparatus used were diverse and included cupping, sweating, bleeding and primitive surgery as well as talismans and neolithic sites, interventions by elves and fairies, holy groves, healing wells, relics of violent death, moon-magic, excreta and herbs. If only to placate the church there were references to healing saints, magi and celestial powers; but in fact these practices bore little relation to the Gospel tradition of healing except that the belief that diseases were caused by malevolent spirits was still widespread. It is interesting to note, though, that the 'white' or beneficient witches and warlocks often used a form of laying on of hands, demanded faith from their patients, and refused direct payments.

This folk tradition proved long-lasting. In the late seventeenth century nine women were executed in the Midlands village of Husband's Bosworth for failing to work a cure for epilepsy. Little more than a hundred years ago two hundred Dorset worshippers assembled on high ground to be cured at a certain phase of the moon. Reptiles' dung was recommended by a leading physician in 1862, and the Lee penny – a typical talisman – was reported to be in use for curing diseased cattle in the early years of the nineteenth century. Some magic springs, as at Bath, have evolved from pagan or Roman shrines through Christian ones to become hydropathic establishments: others, like Glastonbury and St Winefride's own at Holywell in Flintshire, have preserved a religious flavour. An exaggerated horror of hydrophobia, together with a belief that it can be prevented by certain stones, is still to be found in

Wales; and elsewhere many still honour a metal-magic
glossed with pseudo-science by carrying copper amulets to
guard against rheumatism or colour-magic by wearing red
flannel to prevent disease.

Healing sects such as the 'White Ladies', too, are believed to practise white witchcraft in rural areas to this
day. It has made little difference to popular belief in any
age that, as Kipling wrote of the medieval herbalists, 'Half
their remedies cured you dead, Most of their teaching
was quite untrue.'

The Christian tradition that 'spiritual' cures could be
worked by the intervention of certain saints – often corresponding to pagan deities – such as St Blaise for diseases
of the throat, St Apollonia for the teeth, St Otilia for the
head, St Lawrence for the back, St Vitus for epilepsy, St
Fillan for madness, St Agatha for the breasts, St Fiacre for
the rectum, St Anthony for erysipelas, St Peregrine for cancer and St Burgarde, St Rochus, St Quirinus and Sts Cosmas and Damian for other organs was not, however, quite
forgotten. From the tenth century onwards, too, contemporary saints again became increasingly often credited
with at least *post mortem* healing powers. Then, in 1215,
Innocent III made medicine (though not surgery) more
respectable by expressing his approval of the healing orders; and these became popular if only because their members were outside the reach of civil law and hence could
not be executed if a patient died, as could their lay colleagues.

Indeed, it became almost a criterion of saintliness that
miraculous cures should be worked at shrines such as those
of St Thomas à Becket or by relics of the departed: to
touch the penknife of the holy blissful martyr, for instance, was to be assured of an easy childbirth. St Elizabeth of Hungary and St Catherine of Siena, too, devoted
their lives to orthodox nursing but were held responsible

for paranormal cures after their death. Typical of a later age when documentation had become more respected than tradition were St Francis Xavier, St Ignatius Loyola, St Philip Neri (who considered that only *some* of his order, the Oratorians, had the charisma of healing) and St Theresa of Avila, who passed the church's newly-formulated process of canonization with the backing of four healing miracles.

Earlier St Bernard of Clairvaux had also been credited with cures, as had St Francis of Assisi who made the curious comment that *he* cured bodies but God cured minds. A particularly interesting case is that of St Vincent Ferrer, perhaps the most distinguished of the preaching friars who travelled Europe in the fifteenth century. Though born in Spain and knowing no other language than his own, he visited almost every part of Europe south of Scandinavia and was understood everywhere in his native tongue. In England, as elsewhere, his touch was believed to cure blindness, deafness and lameness, and he may have been the first since the apostolic age to hold services specifically devoted to healing.

But by that time another form of paranormal healing had become popular, particularly in Britain. So far we have considered *only* priests and physicians; but whether in pharaonic Egypt or in the societies of Africa where witchcraft was prevalent, there was often a third office which combined some of the powers of both. This was the office of the tribal sovereign, whose power was more than temporal and who might even inherit the divine privilege of healing by touch.

The belief that a king – or even a queen – was in some degree a priest and in some degree greater than a priest was never confined to the world of Prester John. It entered the Greco-Roman tradition from the East, so that not only King Pyrrhus of Epirus (who cured colic by the highly individual method of the laying on of *toes*) but also such cynics as the emperor Vespasian were popularly believed to possess healing qualities; and it spread even to Iceland, where King Olaf is said to have practised healing in the time of the Eddas. It was held, too, that Clovis, the first Christian king of France, received healing powers from God in the fifth century and passed them on to his successors – most notably Robert the Pious and St Louis, at whose tomb miracles were said to have occurred until the period of the French Revolution. In these later times the king laid on hands whilst saying '*Le roi te touche*: *Dieu te guerisse,*' a phrase reminiscent of the surgeon Ambroise Paré.

But nowhere did this belief gain so much power as in Britain. Here the monarch first credited with healing abilities (at least by William of Malmesbury) was also a saint in his own right, Edward the Confessor. According to one tradition the power was linked with the sapphire in his ring which still forms part of the crown jewels, but a more general belief was that all Christian kings derived a healing gift from the act of anointment performed at their crowning. This anointing, with oil compounded from a secret formula and contained in an eagle-shaped ampulla, still survives in the ritual of the coronation of the sovereigns of Great Britain; and through it the recipient was held to inherit *ex officio* powers of healing which were no more dependent upon his personal qualities than the ability of a priest to conduct valid sacraments was dependent upon his human worthiness.

The belief was so firmly established by the time of the Norman Conquest that later English chroniclers felt able to claim that the French crown had only acquired its therapeutic powers through association with the British one. At first the ability to heal was vaguely generalized. But from Plantagenet times onward it became divided into two main streams.

The first of these was concerned with the blessing of rings and coins which were held to cure (and to act as prophylactics against) lameness, leprosy, ulcers, epilepsy, gout and cramp, and even to act as aphrodisiacs: these 'touch pieces' and 'king's riches' came into such demand all over Europe that they were debased from gold to silver and at last to copper. In the second stream were cures achieved by the sovereign's direct touch (which might be efficacious even after his death), 'stroking', or making the sign of the cross over the sufferer. This was one method used for treating the 'king's evil' or scrofula – a then common condition of the skin, related to the widespread malnutrition of the times, which in the words of Shakespeare made sufferers 'swollen and ulcerous, pitiful to the eye, the mere despair of surgery'.

Far from being diminished by the Reformation, the curative powers of the sovereigns of Britain (though now denied by Roman Catholic authorities) were held by Tudor historians to endorse both the divine right to rule and the truth of Protestant principles: furthermore, the public had now no healing shrines to turn to. Elizabeth I certainly did not care much for the practice, but it was revived by the witch-hunting and propagandist James I and enthusiastically endorsed by Charles I, the 'king and martyr', whose shirt (still preserved at Ashburnham, Sussex) was believed to be responsible for cures until a little over a century ago. In the interregnum the Cavaliers claimed that Cromwell tried to cure lameness and other defects by similar means, and that his failure was a proof of divine disapproval. But under Charles II royal healing more than recovered its reputation.

In special services held on Good Fridays or during smaller weekly meetings, Charles treated an average of some five thousand sufferers a year. Measures had to be adopted to regulate the crowds which flocked to be cured, and on more than one occasion patients were killed in the crush despite a system of admission by ticket. But British records appear to have been broken in 1686, when on Easter Sunday alone Louis XIV of France ministered to nearly one thousand six hundred; and the king of Spain also drew huge crowds of sufferers. Royal healing, indeed, reached its peak of popularity towards the end of the seventeenth century; and though there were some like Pepys who disapproved of it on religious or aesthetic grounds, even the most sceptical and anti-royalist of physicians was convinced of the validity of many cures. A register of these was indeed kept open for public inspection. Since the practice also contained elements of many different schools of paranormal healing, it is particularly disappointing to note that never was scrofula more prevalent in Europe than at this time.

A service for royal healing dating back to the reign of Henry VII was still included in the Anglican prayer book of 1719: Dr Johnson was, on his physician's advice but apparently without benefit, touched as a two-year-old child by Queen Anne: and the practice was continued by the exiled Stuarts until 1780. But perhaps William III should be allowed the last word on the subject. As he wearily treated a sufferer by words and gestures in which he himself had no faith he is reported to have said, 'God give you better health – and more sense.'

Royal healing, however, forms only a backwater of Renaissance philosophy. More numerous even than its adherents were those who were not satisfied by faith in a mere mortal, however powerful, and who preferred phenomena on a grander scale – the astrologers and their followers. Essentially these believed (as they continue to believe) that human personalities and events were ruled by the conjunction of certain stars and planets: but from its origin (probably in Egypt) about 500 BC, astrology had grown to embrace a mass of disparate creeds, ranging from alchemy to Pythagoran number-magic and the Aristotelian theory of elements, and even its medical side combined realistic anatomy with a belief in the Galenic humours. The full history of this system has filled many books: in summary one can only suggest that astrology leaves us with the same impression as does the philosophy of the Platonic Greeks – that man's intelligence and desire for order had functioned beyond the experiential data available to him.

At its zenith in the early sixteenth century astrology was stronger than science or medicine: men of the calibre of St Albert, Paracelsus and van Helmont fell under its influence. It was stronger than the church, which had always regarded it with ambivalence: now even the Pope had his own astrologer. And inevitably the practitioners of the medical branch of astrology, with their systems of diagnosis, treatment and prognosis and their convictions that (for instance) jaundice would be cured by a decoction of camomile gathered on a Sunday when Virgo was in the house of the sun, were even less inclined towards paranormal healing than were the few physicians who remained aloof from astrology.

We are now in the midst of the complex revolution which took place in European (and particularly northwestern European) thought around 1600. The scientific Renaissance and the Reformation are indeed only complementary aspects of this period of change. Under the influence of the former, belief in astrology and in the more primitive forms of magic slowly decreased, though some of these were given a new and pseudo-scientific shape as in the 'sympathetic' healing of Sir Kenelm Digby, which was favoured by Descartes and Mme de Sevigné — but whose roots went back through Anglo-Saxon weapon-salves to African magic. Such beliefs have not, in fact, wholly vanished even in the most highly evolved countries, and they remain common in the Near East.

Meanwhile, for several centuries spanning the Reformation and Counter-Reformation, the Catholic healing shrines were comparatively disregarded. Relatively few new saints were created and even exorcism tended to fall into disuse – though it was never completely discontinued nor even confined to the religious, for early in the present century the American physician Carl Wickland believed psychosis to be due to possession and therefore curable by exorcism. But if in general the church appeared more involved in political than in spiritual or charitable activities, the decline or temporary eclipse of old beliefs by no means put an end to paranormal healing. Medical science in Europe had begun its revival at Salerno in the twelfth century, but it was not yet ready to provide an alternative to the therapy of mysticism. A gap was waiting to be filled; and this was done by two main groups.

On the one hand, though some of the new Protestant sects in the Calvinist tradition were even more fatalistic than were the Mosaic Jews or the fifth-century church in their insistence that sickness was God's pre-ordained punishment for original sin, others tried to meet their Master's challenge with regard to healing. Martin Luther, for instance, believed that to the strong in faith no disease was incurable and was even to gain a posthumous reputation as a healing 'saint'. But on the other hand there were men, just as typical of the scientific and the theological revolution, to whom creeds were largely incidental and to whom the challenge was to heal pragmatically. It was left mainly to members of this priesthood of the laity to carry on, for nearly two and a half centuries, the tradition of paranormal healing.

CHAPTER TWO

## From the Stroker to the Magnetist

THE history of the careers, claims and possible cures of the individual healers who practised in the later seventeenth, eighteenth and earlier nineteenth centuries has yet to be written in full. But an excellent series of articles published by the late Fr Herbert Thurston, S.J., in the Roman Catholic review *The Month* more than thirty-five years ago, does much to fill the gap, and I have drawn heavily upon this material in the first part of the present chapter. I should note that *The Month* is a most reputable critical review and that Fr Thurston was regarded as an expert in paranormal and pseudo-paranormal phenomena. The conclusion which he himself drew from the evidence provided by the healers first considered here was that it pointed to 'the existence of some natural faculty in certain individuals of influencing, with or without contact, not only the minds but the physical conditions and reactions of people brought into relation with them'.

The first of the documented post-Reformation healers is to be found in Commonwealth Britain. One must say 'Britain' rather than 'England' here, for Valentine Greatrakes, though of English parentage, had been rewarded with an Irish magistracy for his services as a lieutenant in the Roundhead cavalry. Born in 1628 and later to be known as 'the Stroker', a puritan though not an extreme one, Greatrakes had led an active life and reached the age of thirty-four before he had 'an impulse or strange persuasion' that he had healing powers. At first, however, he treated only the king's evil, which during the interregnum was believed (at least by royalists) to be on the increase because the royal touch was no longer available.

So Greatrakes stroked sufferers with his hands and 'desired God, out of His abundant mercy, to heal them; Who, blessed be His name, heard my prayer, and delivered them, so that few or none, unless those whose bones were infected or eaten, returned without their cure'. Some healings, though, took up to six weeks to complete, and Greatrakes' own wife remained sceptical of his abilities.

Then, after two or three years, the Stroker was persuaded to the conviction that he could also cure agues. Here, too, he appeared successful, and so he progressed to the treatment of many other diseases. His technique was to 'squeeze' an ailment – or its symptoms – to an extremity of the body, and then out of it, with a 'warm and balsamic touch'. By 1665 Greatrakes was conducting a regular 'surgery' for twelve hours a day three days a week, and had been forced to build extensions to his house to accommodate the waiting sufferers. A man of independent means, he rarely accepted payment for his services.

Although he was reprimanded by an ecclesiastical court the Stroker's reputation spread to London, and whole shiploads of sufferers soon crossed the Irish Sea. In England, even men of the calibre of Andrew Marvell, John Evelyn and Robert Boyle – the 'sceptical chemist' and reviser of the pharmacopoeia, though a believer in witchcraft – were impressed by his powers. Greatrakes did not claim to be infallible (the astronomer Flamsteed being one of his failures): there were also some whose pains 'returned after they thought themselves well recovered'. But there is reliable documentation for cures of ailments ranging from blindness to fistulas, and Greatrakes' modesty and sincerity were never questioned. More than one observer remarked on the impression he gave of strength combined with gentleness.

By 1667 the Stroker's powers were fading as mysteriously as they had grown. But despite the brevity of his 'ministry' (and it is hard, when writing of such men, to decide whether to employ the vocabulary of medicine or of religion) details of it have survived the passing of over three centuries. It was noted, for example, that cynics were cured as easily as believers, and that, when touched, sufferers' limbs often became 'so cold and insensible that the patient would not feel the deepest prick of a pin'. An ecclesiastic who saw Greatrakes lay hands upon nearly a thousand sufferers summed up cautiously by saying 'there is something in it more than ordinary, but I am convinced it is not miraculous', and others used question-begging phrases such as 'a sanitative contagion'. The Stroker himself remained puzzled by his powers, but inclined to the view that some form of exorcism was involved.

The next outstanding healer was a very different character – a poor, dirty, ignorant old Cheshire woman known as Bridget Bostock. In 1748, when she was about seventy years old, Bridget's reputation suddenly spread: it is one of the minor mysteries associated with this subject that the early stages of a healer's career are often unrecorded. A witness at that time stated that 'people come from sixty miles around [in carriages] and the poor came by cart loads'. Several villagers made an income simply from holding the horses of patients, and at her peak the 'Healer of Coppenhall' was treating seven hundred sufferers daily.

The cures attributed to this 'great doctress' are even less well-attested than those of other practitioners of the past; but it was claimed that they included hysteria, shortness of breath, dropsy, palsy and 'in short' (as a commentator wrote) 'almost everything'. Her method was to fast during 'surgery' hours and to stroke or anoint patients with her saliva as well as to pray briefly for them. Saliva itself had been used therapeutically by Christ and Vespasian, was mentioned by Pliny, and had earlier been approved by the Egyptians.

'The poor, the rich, the lame, the blind and the deaf all pray for her and bless her' the account continues, 'but the doctors curse her.' But there was no suggestion, even from the most disapproving, that Bridget Bostock (whose wages as a housekeeper were 35s. a year) ever took a penny for her therapeutic services.

Meanwhile in 1727 – or just about a century after the birth of Greatrakes – Johann Joseph Gassner had been born in western Austria. He received a Jesuit education and was ordained as a priest in the Roman church, but the ill-health manifested by headaches, gastric disturbances and the chest pains which he attributed to consumption interfered with his parochial duties. Gassner noticed that his symptoms were at their worst when he was celebrating Mass, and concluded that the Devil was trying to take possession of him. He fought his enemy by self-exorcism, and after some success formed the belief that much human illness (though not all, for he recognized certain 'natural' diseases which he refused to treat) was caused by diabolic interference.

Years passed before Fr Gassner felt ready to cast out demons from others; but by 1774, when he was forty-seven, his healing activities had taken precedence over all other claims on his time. In fact, these pursuits were beginning to cause some scandal in the church, if only because Gassner used a shortened form of exorcism of his own invention instead of the official ritual of bell, book and candle. But he was fortunate in finding a patron in the Bishop of Regensburg, and afterwards he treated, every month, some two thousand sufferers of all persuasions, and achieved immediate relief from symptoms for a high proportion of them.

Gassner, however, was not satisfied with healing for its own sake and regarded his successes as evidence of the validity of his faith. At elaborate mass meetings at Ellwangen he combined Roman ritual with evangelical showmanship, added a personal philosophy of possession with its own arcane vocabulary, and preached in the Holy Name of Jesus. One of his demonstrations was to order the demon in his patient to reproduce the symptoms of an epileptic fit. More often than not the patient would fall writhing to the ground, even if the command had been given in Latin and he did not understand that language. At Gassner's orders his subjects would laugh, weep, become aggressive, perform tricks and – most significantly – fall into a deep trance in which they would still obey his instructions.

With our present knowledge it is not difficult to recognize that this Austrian priest was, unknown to himself, an important figure in the history of the relationship between mind and body. But from the point of view of healing the evidence of lasting cures received at his hands is slight, consisting only of a few cases of diseases of a rheumatic type. And although Gassner could (to his own satisfaction at least) conquer the Devil, he could not escape the deep blue sea of Holy Church. The scientists and medical men of his day were divided in their opinions – as nearly one hundred lengthy contemporary monographs witness – though they were less critical in approach than those who had tried to assess the value of the work of Greatrakes a century before. But there was no place for parlour tricks within the church, even when they were performed by a bishop's protégé. After a period of renown even briefer than that of the Irish Stroker, Gassner was forbidden to practise.

It is probably coincidental that the next major figure was also of German origin; for an interest in faith healing was, and is, almost ubiquitous and its practitioners in the eighteenth century came from every populous western country except the most strongly theocratic ones. Furthermore, Prince Alexander Leopold Franz Emmerich von Hohenlohe-Waldenburg-Schillingfürst differed yet again in type from the retired military man, the ignorant peasant and the country parson whom we have met so far. Born in Würtemberg in 1794, he was a minor aristocrat renowned in his youth for his piety and ordained a priest in the Roman Catholic church shortly after he came of age. Unlike his predecessors he discovered his healing powers early in life after a series of recorded incidents.

One of the Reverend Prince von Hohenlohe's neighbours was a devout peasant named Martin Michel who believed that he had cured himself of a chronic illness by intensive prayer and had then undertaken a healing mission. Michel arranged for the prince to preach at a church whose incumbent was related to him; but when the time for the service came von Hohenlohe was suffering from an acute infection. Priest and peasant prayed together: Michel massaged the prince's throat: and there was a sudden and complete cure.

Shortly after this incident von Hohenlohe heard of a young princess, Mathilde von Schwartzenberg, who had for eight years been crippled by paralysis. On the 21 June 1821, while he was saying his daily Mass, the prince was seized by the idea that, if only she would put her trust in God, the disease which had baffled physicians from all over Europe would be cured. The same day he went to see the princess, taking Michel with him. The two men prayed fervently by her bedside, and the prince felt himself compelled to say 'In the name of Jesus Christ, arise and walk.' The girl undid the straps of the special bed which she used, rose to her feet, and walked across the room.

The status of the protagonists added local interest to the event, and within a few days von Hohenlohe had dozens of sufferers calling upon him. At first he seems to have operated mainly by simple prayer, claiming no personal gifts and crediting favourable results to the patient's faith rather than to his own. But soon he turned to the techniques of 'stroking', laying on of hands or directly commanding the patient to be cured. Meanwhile, the humble Michel who had 'converted' von Hohenlohe also continued to heal.

The priest-prince himself, who was still aged only twenty-seven, was not only besieged by crowds demanding cures. He also became a focus of attention for angry physicians – by this time organized into a profession more self-confident and arrogant than previously – who saw their means of livelihood diminishing. Some of these, even in Catholic Bavaria, also had an idealistic contempt for 'superstition'; and the church was in its usual ambivalent position when confronted by a junior priest popularly regarded as a saint.

Von Hohenlohe was in fact challenged by the medical profession to carry out an experiment on eighteen hospitalized patients. He took up the challenge but, in sharp contrast to the hundred per cent successes recorded elsewhere, no improvement at all was observed. Yet, curiously enough, it was not von Hohenlohe but Michel who was, within a month or so, forbidden to practise anywhere in Bavaria.

The priest, however, remained loyal to the friend who – probably because of his lower rank – had become the scapegoat. He too gave up 'contact' healing for a time and adopted instead a new practice. This was to prove significant in the future, and indeed (if the phrase can be used in connexion with so disputable a subject as faith healing) marked a technical advance.

No law, von Hohenlohe argued, could regulate private prayer. So, at the end of 1821, he made it known that at certain hours he would be saying a special Mass for the sick. He urged the suffering to join their prayers with his at such times: those who wrote to him, he promised, would be mentioned by name in his own orisons. And so this prince and priest of the early nineteenth century founded not only the cult of 'absent healing' but also the custom of synchronized private prayer more typical of our own age of exact time-keeping.

Von Hohenlohe's reputation had by now spread not only throughout the continent of Europe but overseas too: in fact, the pressure of his work forced him to employ a fellow-cleric – himself a healer – as his secretary and assistant. Among the patients he treated by absent healing was a Roman Catholic novice nun named Barbara O'Connor, who lived near Chelmsford and was suffering from an infection which had begun with a poisoned thumb and later extended to her whole arm and shoulder. Conventional medical treatment for eighteen months had proved unsuccessful and by early 1822 the girl's wrist was fifteen inches in circumference: her fingers looked to the eyes of the convent's physician, a Protestant, 'ready to burst': and even in that insanitary age the stench of decay was so offensive that Miss O'Connor's room had special ventilation.

On 2 May 1822 the surgeons advised amputation. Next day, however, von Hohenlohe remembered the sufferer while he was saying Mass at Bamberg, some thousand miles away. As his service came to an end at its previously announced time it was noticed that the swelling of the wrist had diminished. By nightfall it was only five inches round, and four days later Barbara O'Connor was well again.

Her physician denied that the cure was miraculous, but nevertheless published a confirmatory account of it. Meanwhile, two similar incidents had been reported from Ireland alone. Shortly afterwards, too, a Frenchwoman living in London was cured of what seems to have been acute nervous indigestion after three 'absent' sessions with the prince.

As a result of all these reports a dispute sprang up in England, which was at that time in a state of bitter religious controversy. The Roman Catholics – in Britain and elsewhere – claimed von Hohenlohe's cures as proof that God had given special powers to their priests. The Protestants, grumbling that superstition seemed the best doctor', could do no better than suggest that the whole thing was a papist plot and that the cures involved deliberate impostures.

Yet perhaps the most remarkable of von Hohenlohe's apparent cures took place in the United States of America. There, on the 10 March 1824, the Roman Catholic sister of the Mayor of Washington, Mrs Anne Mattingly, was suffering from almost total paralysis. Intercession for her was to take place (according to one of von Hohenlohe's common practices) at the end of a nine-day period of devotion, and during this novena Mrs Mattingly's condition had so deteriorated that she was twice thought to have died. She was, in the opinion of 'more than ten respectable persons', again at the point of death on the night before her attempted cure. This, because of the difference of times, was arranged for 3.30 in the morning, with a Mass being said at the sick-bed to coincide with von Hohenlohe's own celebration in Europe.

Immediately after taking communion Mrs Mattingly is reported not only to have lifted her arms and cried out in prayer – both of which she had been unable to do for weeks – but also to have asked for her clothes, dressed herself, knelt to pray, and finally walked across the room. Later that morning she 'took as much food as she had taken for the space of six months previous', received hundreds of visitors and 'from the ghastly, emaciated, livid semblance of a dying person [was] restored to an angelic countenance. All the physicians who attended her solemnly declared that the nature of her distemper was entirely out of reach of medical assistance', continues the report. This was written by a fellow Roman Catholic; but it should not be forgotten that the official church was still sceptical of von Hohenlohe's claims and that his clerical biographer, writing nearly a century later, *remained* sceptical of them.

The case of Mrs Mattingly seems to have been the last of the prince's well-publicized cures before, in the same year of 1824, he was transferred to Hungary. He never, however, abandoned his healing vocation, and twenty years later was seeing some eight thousand sufferers yearly. By that time the church had accepted the dual role of priest and healer; in 1844, five years before his death at the age of fifty-five, von Hohenlohe had been consecrated an auxiliary bishop.

The next generation of healers perhaps belongs to a different tradition. But there are three transitional figures who may be included in the present company. The first of these – and in some ways the strangest of all healers – was the Zouave Jacob.

Born in central France in 1828, and probably of Jewish ancestry, Jacob first found fame as a trombonist in the military band of the Zouaves. He then became interested in the new creed of Spiritualism, but did not profess any faith in a personal God. (Later he apparently came to believe less in spirits and more in a divinity, and even adopted such Christian phrases as 'arise and walk'.) He probably began his work of healing while serving in the Crimea and Algeria; but it was not until he was stationed in Châlons in the mid-1860s that his activities were reported in the press, with the result that the public began to besiege his tent to a degree which prejudiced good order and military discipline.

A transfer to Versailles only made matters worse, for the Zouave found an enthusiastic patron in Paris and at a house in the Rue de la Roquette 'crowds of crippled and diseased humanity pressed into the courtyard' and the police 'were always at hand to keep order'. Jacob's discharge from the army at the age of thirty-nine inevitably followed.

The Zouave not only refused to charge for his 'boons' but declined free-will offerings, even when it was requested that the money should be devoted to healing the poor. (His father however, who now acted as his business manager, did not object to making small sums out of souvenirs, and Jacob himself earned an income from his publications.) He was in fact a man of spiky independence – 'a most intractable, disagreeable fellow, with a sort of conceit about him which must much impede his work', as one who counted himself a friend wrote. If his reputation continued to increase it was not through any personal charm – nor, indeed, because he hawked comfortable and attractive theories.

For throughout his ministry Jacob protested that he had no clue as to the source of his powers, and he did not claim that they were in any way supernatural. Furthermore, though he believed he had cured 'all sorts of diseases', he did not regard himself as invariably successful with any one type. His methods varied, one of them consisting of simply looking at a patient. (An English journalist thought that he had a trance-like carriage and staring eyes.) In some cases the cure was immediate, in others several visits were needed, and yet others were dismissed with the words 'I can do nothing for your disease.'

For Jacob arrived at his own diagnoses and did not ask his patients about their complaints. On occasion he might treat a whole roomful of cripples with a general command to be well – which, according to the reporter, was successful in every instance. But on one point he was positive: he could do nothing unless he was in the same room as the sufferer.

Jacob had at least one spectacular success. But he also – as he readily admitted – had his failures; and these, combined with a hostility from the medical and clerical professions which was fully reciprocated, led to his fall from favour. Although his healing activities continued up to his death just before the outbreak of World War I, he became in his last years a health crank, fulminating against alcohol and (in contrast with the agnosticism which characterized his prime) ascribing his powers to 'the spirits of white magnetism'.

This word 'magnetism' is historically significant and leads us into new country. We have seen how, in the 1770s Fr Gassner was becoming a public figure, but another central European who had come under Jesuit influence made a more original announcement in the same decade. He was Friedrich Anton Mesmer, who had been born close to Lake Konstanz in 1734, qualified as a physician, interested himself (and obtained one of his four doctorates) in astrology, and in Vienna had been influenced by an unbalanced astronomer and student of the paranormal, Fr Maximilian Hell. Mesmer, being himself of unstable personality, inevitably quarrelled with his tutor before long. But in the meantime he had promulgated the idea of 'animal magnetism'.

At least since classical (and probably since Egyptian) times it had been known that if one person could capture the attention of another to a sufficiently intense degree – for instance, through the rhythmic movement of a light – then it was possible to lull him into a state which may loosely be called a 'trance'. In this state certain of the subject's faculties, including self-control, were suppressed and others, such as the ability to bear pain, were enhanced. Abnormal conditions of various kinds could be induced by command alone, and suggestions could be implanted which would outlast the trance.

In medieval Europe this knowledge had passed into the realm of witchcraft. It is to Mesmer's credit that he brought it into the light again, even if he did so in a most unfortunate way and into a decidedly overcast light. For it has been said of Anton Mesmer that, like Christopher Columbus, he discovered a new world – and completely mistook its nature.

According to Mesmer, the universe was united in an 'aestheric continuum' or gas, which was dominated by magnetic forces whose disturbance was the sole cause of all disease. Since the stars were part of this continuum, then astrology was a reasonable concept. Mesmer also thought that the human mind could modify this balance through the medium of induced trance, and his early experiments in healing were claimed to be as successful as those of any previous practitioner. They were also directed at the types of disorder – convulsions and paralyses, hysteria and minor nervous aches, blindness and 'congestions' of the liver and spleen – with which earlier healers had been successful.

Mesmer, though a gamekeeper's son, married a rich widow; and this, allied to his social and musical gifts (his salon was frequented by Mozart and Haydn) helped him to build up a large and influential practice in Vienna and to establish his own hospital. But it was not to last. One of his patients, a neurotic eighteen-year-old girl named Maria Paradies, seems to have recovered her sight under the elaborate gestures of Mesmer's hands and to have gone on to fall in love with him. This *scandale* – an early example of the danger of 'transference' which has become well recognized by modern psychologists – provided the physicians of the Vienna school (at that time extremely orthodox and influential) with an excuse to suppress his practice in 1778. The official reason given, however, was that Mesmer was an imposter. There were also rumours, not unsupported by the evidence, that some of his less critically ill patients had deteriorated under his treatment and even become insane.

Certainly the surroundings which Mesmer devised would have done credit to an oriental sorcerer. In a large room well supplied with mirrors, flowers, stained glass and incense, sufferers were put into a receptive frame of mind by soft music. In the centre was a tub, filled with iron filings, from which protruded rods: round this the patients sat in silent circles, holding either the ends of the rods or each others' hands. At the critical moment the 'magnetist' himself came in, dressed in a lilac silk robe and holding yet another iron rod. He then passed round the circle, staring into his patients' eyes, touching them or making passes over them.

Meanwhile, Mesmer had found time to investigate the work of Gassner himself. His verdict was that the priest was neither a divine miracle-worker nor a fraud but 'a man of good faith but of excessive zeal' and 'a tool of Nature'. The Austrian, he considered, was one whose earlier accidental discovery of some of Mesmer's own techniques had enabled him to work temporary cures.

Re-established in fashionable Paris, and backed by the interest of Marie Antoinette, Mesmer published his *Dissertation on Animal Magnetism*. Like many such theses, this is an almost incomprehensible *mélange* of arbitrary assumptions and circular logic (the author concludes with no fewer than twenty-seven very questionable 'assertions'), suggestive of a paranoid and egotistical personality. But with this work Mesmer built up a new reputation, and his claims eventually had to be investigated, at the command of Louis XVI, by a panel which included such figures as Benjamin Franklin, Lavoisier and Dr Guillotin. This appears to be the first attempt at an independent investigation of the claims of a paranormal healer.

In 1784 the commission unanimously reported that Mesmer's successes, though many of them could be substantiated, derived from the suggestibility of his patients. In particular his theories of magnetism should not be taken seriously. 'It is impossible not to admit,' they wrote, 'that some great force acts upon and masters the patients.' But, they continued, 'this force appears to reside in the magnetiser'. Some sufferers, they also noted, were adversely affected. This verdict resulted in Mesmer withdrawing once again into the shadows: after a thirty-year retirement spent mostly in Switzerland he died in 1815 at the age of eighty.

Mesmer's confusion of vocabulary is deplorable, considering that over two centuries had passed since William Gilbert had explained the behaviour of material magnets – and, indeed, made magnetism one of the first of the sciences to be set on a systematic basis. Even Paracelsus and van Helmont had recognized the power of the lodestone as a physical one, though they also used the term 'magnetism' to imply an occult method of extracting disease and Baptista Porta and others had, about 1600, claimed that magnets had healing powers. It is possible to see in this survival of superstition not only the quest for the philosopher's panacea but also the very ancient belief in the magical powers of iron, though Mesmer himself – who began by dosing his patients with chalybeates and progressed to 'magnetizing' water, trees, musical instruments such as his favourite glass harmonica (which had, ironically, been invented by Franklin), his patients' clothes, the plates off which they ate and even the air they breathed – eventually recognized that his methods had nothing to do with physical magnetism. He also abandoned the use which at one time he had made of electrical machines, and after his death several of his disciples tried to modernize his ideas still further. Puységur, for instance, observed Mesmerically-induced trances more clinically and can be regarded as a link with present-day psychology.

Mesmer's less sophisticated admirers, however, were reluctant to sever such links with the physical sciences. A connexion between the mysterious forces of disease and the mysterious-seeming ones of electricity and magnetism appealed to physicians and their patients alike in the romantic climate of the 'Age of Enlightenment'. And – so curious are the links between orthodox and unorthodox medicine – the passage of a magnet, when accompanied by some theatrical gestures, appeared at first sight to be at least as likely to effect a cure as did an injection of the pus of diseased cows (which caused a similar controversy at the start of the nineteenth century) seem a possible prophylactic against smallpox.

Mesmer lived at a period when any type of puzzling behaviour tended to be 'explained' by attributing it to yet more mysterious miasmas and emanations and when the word 'aether' was used to answer many problems. But he remained immensely influential at least until 1841, when James Braid not only gave 'animal magnetism' or 'Mesmerism' its new name of 'hypnotism' but also set it on a more rational basis. Even half a century or more later, however, hypnosis was still evoking that aura of the occult which is associated with the name of Svengali, and the oldest generation of orthodox physicians (who had lived through the age of Koch and Lister and had seen the rule that theories must follow after facts accepted into medicine) had barely expunged the word 'magnetism' from their vocabulary.

Indeed, nearly fifty years after *that* an unorthodox

'magnetic' healer named E. Ellman was fashionable in London, whilst in Austria Valentin Zeileis was blending Buddhism with a pseudo-scientific neo-mesmerism (which involved such techniques as 'the passage of electric rays through precious stones') and attracting thousands of patients a day to his 'laboratory' in the medieval castle of Gallspach. The vocabulary, at least, of mesmerism remains widespread in contemporary occult literature; and the leading contemporary Italian healer, d'Angelo, also calls himself a 'magnetizer'.

In summary, Mesmer's influence showed itself in three separate ways. It encouraged men such as Elisha Perkins, the inventor of bi-metallic 'tractors' which were stroked over diseased organs, in their use of magnets and coils in attempts to cure organic diseases – attempts which proved no more effective than those of the contemporary 'pneumatic' therapy. It invaded the medical thoughts of the earlier nineteenth century, challenging but unabsorbed, rather as the theories of the Austrian students of the mind were to trouble conventional medicine in the early years of the present one. And it gave another word, another weapon, to the unorthodox healers who confused animal with physical magnetism and who have not yet left us.

One of the latter is worthy of note, even though – unlike virtually every other figure mentioned in this book – he was an undoubted quack in the sense that he did not believe in his own claims and deliberately deceived the public for financial gain. This was James Graham, a Scot with a smattering of medical knowledge who was born in 1745 and who, a few years after Mesmer had captured public attention, opened a grandiose 'Temple of Health' in the newly built Adelphi, London. He was fortunate in his timing, for the Georgian fashionable world had become disillusioned with the orthodox medicine of the time, and men of the calibre of Chesterfield, Gibbon and

Fielding preferred the attentions of such charlatans as the failed drysalter Joshua ('Spot') Ward.

Graham's shrine boasted 'electrical and other scientific appurtenances'; but the centre of attention was a 'Grand Celestial Bed', twelve feet by nine, which was supported on forty columns, attended by the future Emma, Lady Hamilton, and reputed to have cost £10,000. It was decorated with glass jewels and images and supplied with music and perfumes – all of these properties having long been associated with the occult. But the bed, it was stressed, owed its main virtue to the 'artificial loadstones' with which it was charged and to the 'magnetic vapours' which surrounded it.

Graham – perhaps borrowing from an earlier charlatan, Count Cagliostro – claimed that this apparatus, like the traditional healing beds of Pistoia and elsewhere, had general therapeutic powers. But he was also one of the first to realize the financial potential of sexual anxiety, and specialized in letting the bed out to childless couples. Not only the conception but the beauty of a future child was guaranteed; and though Graham professed that his real interest lay in the improvement of the race he worked his price up from 50 guineas a night to 500 guineas – a figure fantastic for the times, and a courtesan's dream. The bed was, after all, 'celebrated from pole to pole and from the rising to the setting of the sun'.

Graham eventually trespassed too far on public credulity, and after switching over to slimming cures he died bankrupt and comparatively young in 1794. But since we are not primarily concerned here with impostors we must return – with a passing reference to the fact that the eighteenth century also saw a revival of Jewish faith healing in the form of the Hasidic movement founded by such prophets as Baal-Shem-Tov – to the main theme of this story.

We have seen how Fr Gassner, and perhaps Greatrakes too, unknowingly used both mass and individual hypnotism to influence their subjects. Later we will see what can and cannot be ascribed to its powers today. For the moment, let us note only that the recognition of Mesmer's forces at the beginning of the nineteenth century is one of the milestones which mark the change from the 200-year-long era of the individual healers to the present age of schools, cults and quasi-scientific explanations of the mystery of paranormal healing.

# CHAPTER THREE

## Latter-Day Healers

So far in this account we have mentioned the New World only briefly. But before the middle of the last century the United States (and in particular New York and New England) became a centre for the varieties of unconventional healing, often associated with esoteric philosophies, which were ironically treated by Henry James and which are today more commonly found in southern California. However, the statistics and data available from this source are of no higher a standard than those quoted in the last chapter, and in many instances even the most elementary biographical facts are missing. Andrew Jackson Davis for example – the ex-cobbler author of thirty lengthy books on a 'harmonial philosophy', whose main tenet seems to have been that there was no such thing as mind but only matter – appeared, as a fully-fledged healer when still in his teens, in Poughkeepsie about 1846. And some twenty years later (after a period, incidentally, in which Florence Nightingale had gained a reputation for more than natural powers of healing), J. R. Newton made a similar appearance in Rhode Island.

There are, however, circumstantial accounts of the work of 'Doctor' Newton, who is reputed to have treated about a quarter of a million sufferers and to have needed special trains to bring them to his meetings. A witness at one of these (who was prejudiced against Newton) admitted that there were numerous cures including one for blindness, but stated that 'organic difficulties such as fractured limbs and distortions from birth [were] not benefited'. 'Diseases originating in a disturbance of the balance of the vital fluids, such as can be traced to a nervous origin', however, 'were cured as by the touch of a magician's wand, and, so far as I could learn, almost without exception.'

In 1868 a free-church parson from Swindon travelled to New York to consult Newton about a neuralgic affliction from which he had suffered for eleven years. Refusing to listen to the patient's case history, Newton poured scalding water over his head, laid hands on him and manipulated the skull until (as the sufferer reported) 'all at once a clicking noise was heard at the top of my spine'. The healer then announced that 'the disturbance of the nerve current has been removed', bade the disease depart in God's name, and intoned 'it is gone, it is gone, it is gone for ever'. So it appeared, for two years later the cleric was still in perfect health. His own attempts at healing, however, met with indifferent results.

The next year another transatlantic visitor found Newton using some form of magnetic apparatus which – together with the hot water treatment – he employed to quieten a mentally ill woman. Tumours and swellings, however, were treated by simple laying on of hands. Newton was indeed an eclectic in his methods, which included the traditional Christian lore of love and prayer, witchcraft – for at times he claimed to be controlled by spirits – hypnotism, electro-magnetic devices, osteopathy, and a hydropathic cure all his own. (He did not, however, deal in herbs as did many of his successors.) This diversity of method prejudiced London against him during a visit in 1870. But even Newton's worst enemies could not allege that he made a profit from his services, though he appeared to have used his richer patients to subsidize the poorer.

Even earlier in the field than Newton – for he had been born in 1802 – was another New England healer, a slight, grey-haired ex-clockmaker named Phineas Parkhurst Quimby. Perhaps less famous in his own right than Newton, Quimby was to prove far more influential, for he was another of those who attempted to elevate a phenomenon into a philosophy: he was a founder of the anti-material-ist and Swedenborgian 'New Thought' of the later nine-teenth century which linked up with Rudolf Steiner's 'anthroposophy'.

At least a dozen American healers prominent in their time were associated with this school, a notable member being Francis Schlatter, who wandered through the south-ern states treating up to 6,000 patients a day and who also conducted a lucrative mail-order trade in blessed handker-chiefs. But Charles and Myrtle Fillmore, both of whom were self-healed invalids, proved most influential through the establishment of 'Silent Unity', an interdenomina-tional Christian healing fellowship with a somewhat in-volved teaching (which includes a faith in 'thought microbes') but an immense following in the United States today. This is in its turn not quite independent of other movements mentioned later in this chapter.

Quimby himself, a man of strong personality though ill-educated and at first considerably influenced by Mesmer, held that his diagnoses and cures were not due to any form of divine or even (though at one stage he made use of a medium) of paranormal intervention, but simply to the faith which his patients had *in him*: this banished pain as did the soothing 'There, there, it doesn't really hurt' of a mother to her child. He went on to assert that all con-ventional medicine was useless (a claim which none of his predecessors had been extreme enough to make) and that disease itself was 'error' and only health was 'truth'.

A typical Quimby statement, for instance, was 'I tell the patient his troubles, and what he thinks is his disease, and my explanation is the cure. If I succeed in correcting his errors I change the fluids in the system, and establish the patient in health. The truth is the cure.' Another was,

'Disease is false reasoning. False reasoning is sickness and Death.'

Quimby holds an important place in the history of unorthodox healing if only because, to meet the demands of his large practice, he not merely revived von Hohenlohe's technique of absent healing but worked by correspondence and circulars. He also forms a bridge between the hypnotic and the purely 'persuasive' approaches. But if his ideas still have currency more than a century later it is due less to Quimby himself than to the remarkable woman who called on him at the International Hotel in Portland, Maine, in October 1862.

Forty-one years old, comparatively wealthy but subliterate, a lifelong invalid in the throes of a second unhappy marriage, Mary A. Morse Baker Glover Patterson Eddy (to give her her final name) underwent at Quimby's hands a treatment reminiscent of Newton's in that it involved a form of water-massage as well as hypnotism. She awoke from her trance cured of the spinal disease which had defeated all orthodox methods – and had also resisted homoeopathy, which Mrs Patterson, with a characteristic scepticism of the claims of others, had rejected with the conclusion that placebos did just as much good. She then climbed a monument to prove her newfound agility and entered on the second half of a life which was to witness no return of that disease, though it was to be far from free of illness.

But there was an extraordinary sequel. Mrs Patterson's parents had been Calvinists; and though she had reacted strongly against this ruthless creed and its insistence that all pain was divine punishment, she retained a residue of extreme nonconformist belief. She hence informed Quimby that her cure was not due to any hypnotic power of his (he had never, incidentally, suggested that it was) but rather to some 'truth of Christ'. Quimby, an agnostic if not an atheist, denied this; and there followed a remarkable period of several years during which Mrs Patterson vehemently popularized Quimby – to whom she had formed a passionate devotion – through lectures and publications which built round his work a theological structure which the healer himself repudiated. At this period she was also an enthusiast for chiropractice.

Quimby died in 1866; and from then on Mrs Patterson suppressed all references to one who had supplied her with even the titles of her books. Like Mesmer following Hell she presented her system as being entirely her own – at least in human terms, for when nine years later she published her *Science and Health* she hinted at direct divine inspiration. In the interim she had supported herself mainly by outright parasitism and had acquired her first disciple, a young man with whom – typically – she soon quarrelled and became involved in complex lawsuits.

Two years after that she married for the third time and, as Mary Baker Eddy, became director of a 'metaphysical college' charging $300 ('cash strictly in advance') for a brief course. She was also on the road to renown as the founder of what – again plagiarizing from Quimby – she termed 'Christian Science'.

The often-revised *Science and Health* remains an egotistical and at times paranoid and demonic book, alternating between the repetitive and the self-contradictory. Familiar words are used in a Pickwickian sense which a glossary does little to elucidate, and idiosyncratic and *ex cathedra* pronouncements of doctrines contrary to all experience are more frequently found than logical arguments. One of the more lucid passages runs: 'You say a boil is painful – but that is impossible, for matter without mind is not painful. The boil simply manifests ... a belief in pain, and this belief is called a boil.' A more typical extract reads: 'The nothingness of nothing is plain;

but we need to understand that error is nothing, and that its nothingness is not saved, but must be demonstrated in order to prove the somethingness . . . of Truth.'

Fortunately we are not here concerned with Mrs Eddy's literary style (which was disposed of by Mark Twain in such phrases as 'showy incoherences' and 'serenities of self-satisfaction'), nor even her theology, so much as with her teachings on health. But even these are sophistical and difficult to summarize. Mrs Eddy regarded herself as the supreme healer and as infallible as Christ: she demanded absolute obedience to her system as to her person, and any failure to be cured must be due to scepticism on the patient's part. She held that faith cures (or, indeed, any cures at all) could only be achieved within her own discipline and claimed numerous miracles, including one worked by preaching to a horse. But she founded no real dynasty of healing, and contrary to general belief the services of 'Christian Scientists' – which began in 1879 – are not primarily curative in aim. There are more than ten thousand specially-licensed (and fee-charging) nurses and practitioners, none of whom has ever achieved particular note; but in addition believers help themselves and others by methods including absent healing.

Nor is the relation between 'Christian Science' and orthodox medicine so firmly prohibitory as is sometimes believed. Mrs Eddy wore spectacles and false teeth and – at least towards the end of her life – used drugs: these were made necessary, she explained, by the 'malicious animal magnetism' of her enemies. She also consulted a physician – though too late – when her husband was dying. She mistrusted nutritional science and even elementary hygiene (though she was a teetotaller and anti-smoker), and wrote that 'The only effect produced by medicine is dependent on mental action'; but in her later years she did not actually forbid it to her disciples, even though some refused all contact with physicians. Medicine might be for the suffering, she thought, as theft for a starving man, a lesser evil. And surgery, she admitted, was best left to surgeons until her methods had been perfected.

How effective were those methods? The followers of 'Christian Science' might have performed a real service had they tabulated and analysed their results, but in their writings and those of their founder (to quote Fr Thurston) all 'names, dates, medical certificates or any details which could lend themselves to investigation are ... withheld'. But such evidence as there is suggests that the practitioners of 'Christian Science' have at best proved no more effective than those of any other unorthodox school, though they can doubtless boast of individual successes where conventional medicine has failed including such spectacular cases as the relief of jaundice in a few minutes. Their tenets have also, beyond doubt, resulted in many unnecessary deaths; and even if we accept that the movement as a whole has been responsible for more good than harm there is little doubt that it would have done more good still without its reverence for a founder who was virtually deified in her own lifetime.

'Mother Mary' – as Mrs Eddy liked to be called, with the added ornamentations of 'Reverend' and 'Doctor' – forbade the celebration of birthdays, which she looked upon as a surrender to the 'illusions of ageing and the passage of time', and denied the reality of death itself. The latter came to her, however, after years of painful decline and just short of her ninetieth birthday. But she had lived to see churches, devoted more to readings from her books than to prayer, founded in her name at the rate of one every four days; and though its period of greatest expansion ended with her life the appeal of 'Christian Science' did not fade after its founder's death as did the teachings of other such latter-day prophetesses as Mme

Blavatsky, Annie Besant and Aimée Semple McPherson. On the contrary, *Science and Health* was to prove one of the most influential texts of its time.

Today there are about three thousand churches and centres of 'Christian Science' and a less extreme 'Jewish Science' movement. The cult is most popular in the United States, but there is a strong representation in Britain too and it is estimated that it has a total of three million adherents in fifty countries. The works of the founder – a woman who, according to Stefan Zweig, was 'scarcely more than half-witted, always ailing and of very dubious character' yet who, despite the rival candidature of John Wesley, has also been called the greatest proselytizer since Mahommet, remain bestsellers: propagandist programmes are broadcast from eight hundred radio stations: and for all its oddities *The Christian Science Monitor* is one of the world's leading newspapers. The cult, appealing mainly to the middle classes, is immensely wealthy, and Mrs Eddy's own estate was assessed at over three million dollars.

To some extent this all-American success story derives from the business abilities of the 'discoverer' and her third husband, and to some extent from the fact that, for all her arrogance, contentiousness and other defects of character and appearance, Mary Baker Eddy could be a sympathetic as well as a domineering personality – confident and hope-inspiring, idealistic and shrewd, a competent lay psychologist with a real compassion for human suffering and an enthusiasm for 'health, life, God'. But despite these factors the spread of her sect is little short of amazing, and it has even inspired learned papers propounding such ideas as that Mrs Eddy was in tune with an expanding society which seemed to have conquered every frontier except the final one of death, or that she was an archetypal mother-image.

For if two adjectives are inappropriate to this philosophy of life (and it is little *less* than a philosophy) they are 'Christian' and 'scientific'. It does not incorporate the principles of any known science nor yet the scientific method; and its cures, even if uncritically accepted, can be explained in non-Christian terms or in Christian ones which owe nothing to Mrs Eddy's personal vision. Nowhere in her works or in those of her disciples is there a sense of cause and effect, and her 'science' helps us neither with verifiable statistics nor with a rationale of faith healing.

If 'Christian Science' is a parody to the scientist, it is anathema to the mainstream Christians who see in it a heresy – a gross if not blasphemous exaggeration of one aspect of their faith to the exclusion of the rest, as well as an attempt to use God for a particular end. According to a Methodist, who refers to the system as a 'maternal autocracy', the creed offers 'Christianity without tears': according to a Roman Catholic commentator, *Science and Health* 'leaves a strong impression that its author considered herself to hold a place in the divine economy not inferior to that of the Blessed Virgin'. Generally, traditional Christian belief accords with common sense in recognizing the darker realities of the flesh – disease and pain and death – and goes beyond common sense in averring the reality of sin. All these are 'illusions' in Mrs Eddy's Manichean dualism: to her, sickness *was* the supreme sin.

In summary, 'Christian Science' appeals to no reason and to only one authority, that of its founder. Its services lack the attraction of either Protestant rhetoric or Catholic ritual. Its philosophy is in essence simple to the point of banality: as developed it is incomprehensible to the simple-minded and ridiculous to the sophisticated. It is without the glamour of occult oriental theosophies or the easy comfort of the offer of an automatic life after death. Above all, it flatly contradicts our most intense everyday experience: for most of us do not need to 'sit on a pin, when it punctures our skin, to dislike what we fancy we feel' in order to reject its Berkeleyan idealism.

Only one thing, indeed, can explain the lasting popularity of the cult, and that is the desperate need of mankind for help which the medical profession cannot give. The history of 'Christian Science' may not throw much light on the occurrence of faith cures. But it certainly underlines the desire for them.

It should be stressed that Mrs Eddy claimed to cure only the *illusion* of sickness and denied the reality of sickness itself – or even that there was a body to be sick. Furthermore, she insisted that it was neither faith nor supernatural intervention but an understanding of 'the Science' which was her therapeutic force. In the strict sense, then, 'Christian Science' does not form a curative discipline at all. For that we must turn to a rival heresy – that of the Spiritualists (or, more correctly, *Spiritists*) whom 'Mother Mary' typically condemned as being both too materialistic and too mystical.

From times long before written history men have tried to communicate with the dead, whether impelled by curiosity, the need for comfort or the desire to be puzzled, amazed or pleasurably frightened. We cannot here examine their claims to have done so with success. What is relevant is that the early nineteenth century saw a great increase – particularly in the Anglo-Saxon countries – in a form of activity which in essence was as old as the most primitive witchcraft cult.

One reason for this resurgence was a decline in public willingness to accept religious authority. The Christian (and particularly the Roman Catholic) church had its own doctrines of the communion of saints involving a link between the living and the dead, but it had set its face against such individual attempts at communication as could be stigmatized as magic. Now, however, the orthodox were on the defensive. And the materialization of spirits seemed to offer the compromise called for by new times – supernatural phenomena which were still subject to controlled observation, a 'scientific' (and very undemanding) religion.

The emergence of Spiritualism from the romantic twilight of table-rapping seances into something resembling a creed can be traced to New York in 1848. Soon after, with the backing of such anti-clerical propagandists as Allan Kardec, it had become such a force on both sides of the Atlantic that the 1860s and 1870s were a golden age of ghosts. But if America took the lead in building the tricks of planchettes and ouija boards into a semi-devotional cult (by 1860 it was estimated that Spiritualism had about thirty thousand mediums and over three million adherents), Britain was first in bringing to bear upon it something resembling a scientific approach.

The Society for Psychical Research was founded in 1882 at the instigation of a group of Cambridge scholars – few of whom, however, had any training in critical observation. Its object was to investigate 'the obscure human faculties', which then included hypnotism as well as a wide range of 'paranormal' behaviour (telepathy, clairvoyance, prevision and so forth) and the mediumistic phenomena of Spiritualism proper. All forms of ghosts, poltergeists, apparitions and manifestations also fell within its province, and indeed came to dominate its early studies.

This society is today a most reputable body, led by men and women of the highest academic standing and approaching problems of this kind in an objective spirit which some might regard as being biased towards scepticism. It has also inspired the formation of similar societies and departments of parapsychology throughout the world. In its lifetime of nearly ninety years it has admittedly thrown comparatively little light on the problems which it set out to investigate; but this is hardly surprising in view of their immense complexity and the very limited resources available to it. Inevitably, too, faith cures have received less attention than have such phenomena as mediumship and telepathy, where no special knowledge on the investigator's part is required.

What *is* surprising is the low level of critical intelligence which was brought to bear on all 'psychic' occurrences in the nineteenth and early twentieth centuries. Scientists of the first rank seem to have been taken in by fake mediums and stage hypnotists, and in the 1890s success at a number-guessing game could lead to the claim that psychical research must be thereafter regarded as 'the handmaiden of religion'. Today, though Spiritualism is officially regarded as a religion in Britain, only one public figure remains committed to it; but throughout the last century there was a continuous stream of men and women distinguished in almost every sphere who proved willing to accept a whole realm of the extraordinary on the strength of a handful of conjuring tricks.

Elizabeth Barrett, Oscar Browning, Oliver Lodge, William Crookes, Edward Marshall Hall, Lord Rayleigh, William Barrett, Robert Owen, W. T. Stead, J. A. Symonds and Arthur Conan Doyle – these were only a few of those convinced by what was at best grossly insufficient evidence. Faced with this list one can but agree with the poet Andrew Lang that 'psychical research does somehow damage and pervert the logical faculty of the human mind' – or turn to another poet, Tennyson, who had remarkable gifts of healing but refused to consider them as either mystical or Christian.

The story of the early attempts to evolve a rationale of

the supernatural has its hilarious and its tragic moments, but we must resist the temptation to follow it further in this book. We are concerned only with the therapeutic aspects of the paranormal, and on these psychical research throws little enough light. Nor is there much to be gleaned from those still less critical believers, the priest-physicians of spiritual healing who held a pioneering international conference in London in 1885 and shortly afterwards set up their 'Bethsea' centres in the capital.

Working in over a thousand groups, such 'spiritual' healers are believed to be responsible for more than nine tenths of the paranormal therapy now practised in the British Isles; and in its history of well over a century the belief that the spirits of the dead can be readily summoned up by the living and can help them has fragmented into many sub-sects. Some, such as the forty-five-year-old 'Seekers', have a Christian flavour and undertake such offices as the laying on of hands. Others, like the Rosicrucians, borrow from oriental religions and involve a belief in reincarnation; yet others are agnostic or in active opposition to all historic creeds.

In all these categories there are some cults in which healing plays a minor part and others (with three major organizations in Britain alone) in which it is so much the centre of existence that their services are attended by tens of thousands of non-Spiritualists in search of health. Nor, in the groups which *are* devoted to healing, does a medium in a more or less trance-like state always attempt to get into touch with a 'control' having the power to send health from the world of the dead. Some do operate in this way, with contacts ranging from Jesus Christ through mythical or historical doctors such as Imhotep or Galen who have 'perfected their art in the beyond' down to unknown Red Indians; but the present tendency is to regard simple prayer, laying on of hands or absent healing as 'safer' and just as effective. Even when spirits are summoned the use of properties such as trumpets and tambourines, and the appearance of ectoplasm, seems to be becoming less frequent.

With more historical than statistical equipment we can now approach faith healing as it has been practised during the present century. From the point of view of organization rather than of creed the healers divide into three main groups. First we find those who operate within the framework of the historic Christian churches and are sometimes ordained ministers of them : these often admit a debt of gratitude to the 'heretics' for stimulating interest in a ministry of healing, just as many physicians recognize the importance of the paranormal healers in the present-day movement away from mechanistic to psychological medicine. But, as Christian attitudes present features of their own, I have preferred to deal with these in more detail in the next chapter and to quote only some individual cases below.

In the second group are the practitioners of 'Christian Science' and of those Spiritualist churches which specialize in therapy – all, in varying degrees, in disagreement with each other. And in yet a third (though these categories are neither quite mutually exclusive nor quite exhaustive) are the successors of the Stroker – the individual healers, some with explanations of their power such as a belief in the casting out of devils and others refusing to commit themselves to any school.

In harmony with the general speeding-up of life (and not, perhaps, without aid from modern methods of publicity and communication) healers of all these types seem to have become more prevalent in the present century, particularly in Britain and the United States. We can hence do no more than select a few representative examples from different schools, either still alive or recently dead.

The Roman church, for example, is currently investigating the lives of several of its recently-deceased members. One of these is Alfred Bessette or Brother Andrew, an unlettered but intensely pious French-Canadian working man who in 1870, when he was twenty-five, became a lay brother and later porter in a Montreal school : from shortly after that date until his death in 1937 at the age of ninety-two a stream of cures at his hands was reported and a large oratory in the city now enshrines his heart. Another – Hubert van Lieshout or Father Eustace – was born in Holland in 1890, worked as a parish priest in a backward area of Brazil and only became a healer in the three years preceding his death in 1943 : his funeral was a national occasion and cures at his graveside are also claimed. (This last phenomenon remains characteristic of Roman Catholic healers : for instance, in the case of the Arab monk Charbel Makhlouf comparatively few cures were claimed before his death in 1898, but from 1950 onwards his grave in the Lebanon became a healing shrine for Moslems as well as Christians.) The Polish Madame Sikora, though a clairvoyante as well as a spiritual healer, was also a pious Roman Catholic; and Padre Pio di Pietralcina, who died in 1968, has been the subject of much discussion.

At the other end of the Christian spectrum from the Roman church we find – though almost exclusively in the United States – those non-denominational, evangelical and fundamentalist ministers whose base is frequently a radio station. Typical of these are (or were) the 'Reverend' Oral Roberts, who is claimed to draw attendances comparable with those of Billy Graham as he tours America holding healing services in a tent with a capacity of eighteen thousand, T. L. Osborn – another hot-gospeller with a world-wide mission who regularly claims cures of a 'miraculous' type – Thomas Wyatt, Franklin Hall and a number of priests serving obscure cults involving the worship of the sun or of snakes. None of these, however, claims quite the powers, therapeutic or otherwise, of the late Father Divine who in his followers' eyes *was* God.

Nearer to orthodoxy, perhaps, was Glenn Clark, the mystical founder of 'Camps Farthest Out'. Also un-attached to any recognized church, though a Christian believer, was Rebecca Beard, an American doctor of medi-cine who was perplexed by the number of remissions of 'incurable' illnesses which she witnessed in her hospital practice. When she herself experienced a spontaneous re-covery from heart disease she attributed the result to her prayers and devoted herself to treating others by spiritual (or, as she termed them, 'psychosomatic') rather than physical means. One of her alleged successes was with can-cer, a disease which she specifically set out to challenge: another, with a spinal condition for which an operation was averted.

Between the extremes of Roman Catholicism and non-denominationalism, almost every church can show mem-bers if not ministers with claims to therapeutic powers. There was, for instance, Mrs Elsie Salmon, the South Afri-can 'Lady in White' who was the wife of a Methodist minister and discovered her gifts accidentally. She believed that Christ inspired her diagnoses and directed a healing current which she could feel flowing through her and en-tering the patient – a phenomenon also reported by Mrs Agnes Sanford, a somewhat sentimental American who came to healing after she had failed (though a minister later succeeded) in curing an abscess in her infant son's ear. The cures credited to Mrs Salmon, which have led to her building up a private shrine of discarded calipers and casts, include cancer, goitres, broken bones and withered limbs (some of these being scheduled for amputation), osteomyelitis, disseminated sclerosis and at least one 'miracle' with a high degree of medical attestation.

The patient in this case was a thirty-year-old woman who had been bed-ridden with tuberculosis of the spine almost all her life and weighed only 2½ stones or 35 pounds. Two days after being touched by Mrs Salmon her deformity disappeared and her body suddenly cracked as it assumed a normal posture and gained seventeen inches in length. Afterwards, although not completely cured, the sufferer was reported as being able to lead a normal life.

In the United States another Methodist, the Rev. Dr Albert Day, was advised by his physician that he would die of an enlarged heart if he did not give up all work: he found prayer a better solution, and went on to establish – with an English helper who believed in his own healing and extrasensory powers – the New Life Healing Clinic in Baltimore. A typical Anglican lay healer was the Canadian Mary Light, and perhaps 'Brother Mandus' of Blackpool also belongs in this category. Among the spiritual healers four women have attracted particular note – the Scottish Margaret Lyon whose 'control' is a Japanese lady and who has links with her national church, the professedly non-Christian Mrs Kingsley Tarpey (of whom it was claimed that even her discarded clothes had curative powers), the clairvoyante Ursula Roberts and Nan MacKenzie: of the men one may cite Gordon Turner, Ronald Beesley, C. A. Simpson and Edward G. Fricker.

The last of these is a burly former glassworks manager of Tottenham who believes that his life has been shaped by the voice of God (though he also has spirit guides) and who claims a number of psychic experiences outside his practice as a healer. In the past twelve years he has treated cancer, spinal diseases and the like in a total of over four thousand patients weekly. Fricker claims ninety per cent successes, though investigations by press reporters showed less spectacular but still impressive results: he also believes that he has acquired a gift of diagnostic 'X-ray sight'. He works to a background of 'pop' music.

But of this school the best known in Britain until recent years was probably William H. Lilley of Leeds, who was born in 1914 of Spiritualist working-class parents. At the age of ten Lilley acquired his first 'guide', a Red Indian who was later joined by a Hindu doctor and yogi and after him by a two-thousand-year-old Egyptian physician. Before he was twenty he claimed to be adept in not only the usual psychic gifts such as clairvoyance but also in the diagnosis and cure of the ailments of patients he had never even met: his first healing – of 'Bright's disease' – in fact took place in 1929 when he was only fifteen. Despite these talents, Lilley was instructed by his Hindu mentor to advise on herbal as well as spiritual cures. Later massage (by a special technique involving high-speed percussion of the spine) and homoeopathic cures were added to his armamentarium.

By 1938 Lilley had achieved a reputation which reached the ears of the chairman of a local engineering concern, Arthur Richards. Sceptical but interested, Richards arranged a trial in which two Leeds physicians were to bring the sealed medical records and a personal possession of each of three of their patients. From these Lilley – or his control – made diagnoses and prognoses which were apparently more accurate than the official medical ones.

This ability to diagnose by paranormal methods, it should be stressed here, is not necessarily associated with the ability to cure. Many faith healers claim no special insight into their patients' ailments, whilst on the other hand there have been those such as the English diagnostician Phoebe Payne and the American Edgar Cayce, who in the 1940s claimed to have carried out some fifteen thousand diagnoses under self-hypnosis, seventy per cent of them proving correct.

Richards was convinced and converted by Lilley's diagnostic performance; and from then on he financed the Spiritualist in his healing mission, provided him with a chapel in his factory, and became a disciple of his methods. Then World War II began. Lilley had no conscientious objections to being conscripted, but claimed that his healing work was of national importance. Early in 1941 he appeared before a tribunal in Manchester to argue his case, and won it after the panel had deliberated for less than two minutes. Probably for the first time in history, 'spiritual' healing had been accorded a legal status. It has also been stated that a London hospital offered Lilley £50 a week to act as a diagnostician, but was refused. In fact, the healer drew only a few pounds weekly for living expenses.

In the early war years Lilley set up other 'sanctuaries' connected with his healing movement called 'Divinity' and acquired further spirit guides whom he used as specialist consultants. During this period he believed that he cured eighty-five per cent of those who consulted him personally and forty-five per cent or more of those whom he treated by absent healing; the figures include organic diseases such as cancer, and numerous cures of animals were also claimed. Many of Lilley's patients were – and remained – sceptics rather than Spiritualists. Lilley differed from most psychic healers in that his cures, which he attributed to the effect of a special kind of ectoplasm, were rarely instantaneous and more often took weeks to become effective.

At his peak, Lilley was running a nursing home in London and treating eighty patients a week; but, as is not uncommon with unorthodox healers of all schools, he subsequently vanished from the scene and I have been unable to trace his activities since 1944 except for a suggestion that he transferred them to South Africa. Meanwhile, however, dozens more names of individual healers in the present or recent past press for inclusion.

There are or were, for instance, William J. Macmillan (who is mentioned later), Harriet Rhodes, Margaret Frayling (a Christian, Spiritualist and mystical disciple of the Fillmores who believed that every disease could be cured 'but by no means every patient'), Millicent Smith, and Ambrose and Olga Worrall. Some of these belong to recognized schools, others have somewhat vague philosophies of their own based on such concepts as 'positive thinking', and others again prefer action to discussion. Their attitudes to both established religion and orthodox medicine include almost every possible nuance from respect to enmity.

In England alone there are probably well over ten thousand psychic healers, including such diverse personalities as a Buddhist practitioner, a retired army officer, a blind man, a London grocer offering healing across a counter, a bacteriologist, a farmer, a yogi clergyman, a former cinema organist, reporters and several civil servants. Others (one of whom claims an eighty per cent success rate) believe they are able to heal animals, and at least one has described the control of plant growth by blessing and cursing. Over two thousand of them are associated in a single body, and the demand for their services is such that some healing centres work on a mass-production basis with sufferers being attended to by adepts of varying degrees of skill. In the United States there are many more, following in the steps of such later nineteenth-century healers as G. O. Barnes the 'Mountain Evangelist' of Kentucky, J. A. Dowie (an eccentric Scots-Australian emigré who believed himself to be a reincarnation of the prophet Elijah and founded Zion City), and E. W. Stanford who claimed to be able to raise the dead; these are apparently encouraged by do-it-yourself courses on the subject. At Wainwright House near New York regular and thoughtful seminars on spiritual healing are held, whilst at the other extreme one American healer believes that the virtues of his touch are communicated to a radio set tuned in to his programme.

There is also a widespread interest in the subject on the continent of Europe, particularly in Switzerland, in Scandinavia and Germany, and in Holland where Margaretha Greet Hofmans was recently the centre of a constitutional crisis. Despite church opposition there are numerous practitioners in Italy too, such as Dr F. Racanelli who claims that his touch is more effective than his medical skills and Achille d'Angelo, the 'Wizard of Naples' who has been said to earn about £75,000 a year from his practice. Maurice Colinon has estimated that there are over forty thousand unorthodox healers in France – though these, it should be pointed out, are predominantly homoeopathic rather than psychic in approach since homoeopathy is almost as popular as 'official' medicine in that country. India still produces healing saints such as Sadhu Sundar Singh, and the shadow of Gandhi was also held to be therapeutic. Even communist China has its own school of paranormal therapy, with 'application to the thought of Mao-Tse-Tung' (i.e., dialectical materialism) having been claimed to prevent infection following severe burns. Russia's only recent candidate, however, appears to have been Rasputin.

Hence any exhaustive study of the subject – which would be further complicated by the thousands of people who believe that they have cured only *themselves* by faith – is impossible. But two contemporary British healers call for a final note here, if only because both are known to me personally and will enter into this account at a later stage. The first of these is Christopher Woodard, perhaps an English equivalent of Dr Beard.

He was born in 1913, the son of a Suffolk priest, and was educated at Lancing and Cambridge. Then (having decided in favour of medicine rather than the church) he entered a London hospital and qualified on the eve of the war. A special interest in athletics led to his specializing in orthopaedics and the psychology of competitive sports: on demobilization from the navy he set up a hospital unit for the treatment of athletic injuries but left it to continue his interest in private practice. As well as providing or- thodox medical services he endeavoured to increase his patients' confidence by affirmation of their good health, by 'willing' them to win sporting events at which he was not present, and by prayers and laying on of hands.

The turning point in Dr Woodard's life, however, came in 1950 when his two-and-a-half-year-old son was struck by cerebro-spinal meningitis. The boy underwent surgery and was not expected to live – or, if he did survive, to re- cover his normal faculties. While he lay critically ill, how- ever, his father organized a crusade of prayer which was led by a friend who was an Anglican priest and also a faith healer: he himself prayed for the dying boy while holding his hand.

A few days later Dr Woodard was told by a 'Christian Science' friend (whose religious beliefs he did not share) that she had received 'guidance' that his son had turned the corner. This proved to be true, and though recovery was slow it was complete. The evidence provided by this incident – and by an earlier 'miracle cure' in which Dr Woodard was involved in his naval days – is perhaps slight; but it appears to have finally persuaded him that he should practise faith healing in parallel with his more orthodox activities.

In his books – which contain some rather curious syllogisms – Dr Woodard reports his own paranormal cures in cases of perforated appendix, road accidents, poliomyelitis, rheumatic fever, nephritis and the 'blue baby' condition: most of his patients had been accorded a grave prognosis but nevertheless had continued treatment by orthodox methods alongside his own. He also admits to several apparent failures.

Theologically, Dr Woodard works along Anglican lines. He begins his consultations with prayers and prefers to act with an ordained priest holding church services. He believes that all disease and pain, but not natural death, is against God's will and therefore curable by prayer, and regards orthodox medical diagnosis and treatment as a temporary stop-gap – though he still employs these himself when his intuition tells him that an attempt at a faith cure would be ineffective. He does, however, recognize the usefulness of healers of persuasions differing from his own, and indeed takes pride in the fact that he suspends all critical faculties in the interest of an eclectic approach to healing.

Dr Woodard seems sympathetic to homoeopathy and its allied arts. He considers that the faith of physician, patient and other parties concerned are all involved in the ideal cure, but concedes that healing can proceed in the absence of some of these. Finally, he is also a believer in 'health' foods and herbs, in signs and omens, and in diabolical possession.

In contrast with Christopher Woodard's fringe Anglicanism is the emphatic Spiritualism of Harry Edwards, who was born in 1893 in London and as a boy dedicated himself to progressive politics. The First World War brought him into contact with oriental religions and also found him carrying out primitive but effective treatment with the aid of the army's medicaments and his own unformulated belief that he could heal.

Demobilized in 1921, Harry Edwards entered the family trade as a printer and stationer with a small shop in Balham. For fourteen years he devoted his spare-time energies to working for the Liberal party, but having failed to win a parliamentary seat in 1935 he sought a new opening for his idealism and interested himself in Spiritualism. Beginning as a sceptic and rationalist – he was, indeed, an amateur conjurer interested in duplicating mediumistic phenomena – he soon became convinced that these did in fact take place without trickery.

At this stage Mr Edwards learned that a friend of a member of his circle was bed-ridden with a diseased lung. In his first attempt at absent healing he had a vision of the patient – who, within a few days, made a remarkable recovery – and at the age of forty Harry Edwards began to believe that he had a gift of healing. This faith was strengthened by two similar successes in the following weeks. He also learnt that he could so attune himself to a patient that his own spirit was projected through space to the bedside – the converse of later occurrences in which, it is claimed, sufferers who did not know that absent healing had been asked for on their behalf 'saw' and 'felt' the healer treat them though he was in fact miles away.

Within months Harry Edwards became first a local and then, through press reports, a national figure. Since the end of the war he has become as famous as any lay healer in his own lifetime, having been for twenty years a household name in Britain and having built up an extensive reputation overseas as well. His 'sanctuary' at Shere, Surrey, is almost as renowned as Lourdes, with which Mr Edwards compares it favourably : he has published a monthly magazine for over seventeen years : and he claims six members of the royal family – which has in general been sympathetic to unorthodox medicine – among his patients.

However, I find some of Mr Edwards' statistics difficult to apprehend. Apart from one claim to have worked ten thousand cures over a period of more than four years (ten thousand out of how many we are not told), and a success rate estimated at various times as being between eighty and ninety per cent for improvements and thirty and forty per cent for complete cures, he writes only in terms of 'thousands', 'many', or 'most'. Further, it is hard to understand how he can give his personal attention to over 600,000 letters a year. Even a staff of twelve typists and several assistants does not alter the fact that this implies a letter being received and read, probably a reply being dictated and signed, and a name being 'offered to the spirits' every twenty seconds of every long working day. The unconventional healer may for good reasons find the follow-up of patients' histories even more difficult than does the conventional one; but more attention to records might well do both Mr Edwards and his cause a service.

Harry Edwards' creed, however, is fairly clear and perhaps as reasonable as that of most theologians. He maintains that there are spiritual laws in the universe which even God would not upset and that hence cures cannot come directly from Him and miracles do not occur. He does, however, claim that at his hands the whole range of 'incurable' diseases, including numerous forms of cancer, has been tamed. In common with other paranormal practitioners, he asserts that these growths can be dissolved in 'spirit operations' and expelled as sweat, vomit or faeces. And the power behind this, he suggests, is the superhuman but not limitless intelligence of the spirits of the dead. Harry Edwards' own favourite controls were formerly Red Indians, but Pasteur and Lord Lister were later added to their number.

Sometimes these may give the passive medium a diagnosis, perhaps in medical terms unfamiliar to him; but this is not necessary for effective healing to take place. Mr Edwards now considers trances and gestures equally unnecessary; and though he undertakes bone manipulation – for which he appears to have a natural gift – he has come to regard absent healing, often without the patient's knowledge that he is under treatment, as *more* effective than direct contact. (This is, of course, the basis of his enormous practice.) Faith on the patient's part he regards as unimportant; and sometimes the healer himself is unaware of the presence of his guides who – unlike the capricious controls usually associated with Spiritualism – appear to be available at all times.

Perhaps a weaker part of Harry Edwards' philosophy is his explanation of why certain attempts at cures are unsuccessful. We must all die sometime, he suggests, and even the spirits cannot reverse ageing. He is also capable of special pleading, as in the case of his failure to prevent his friend, the medium Jack Webber, from dying prematurely and mysteriously. But he does not attempt to explain why some of his cures seem immediate and 'miraculous' (and there are good witnesses to a number in this class) while others are slow or followed by relapse. Others too are partial, as in the case of the baby born with two deformed feet of which – at least for a while – only one was rectified.

Harry Edwards shows some animosity towards the medical profession for not taking his own work seriously, but recognizes the wisdom of his patients who call in medical and surgical help as a supplement to his ministrations. He is inclined to believe in the value of both herbalism and of 'etheric vibrations', but claims that though they are themselves curative these function at a different level from true spiritual healing. He concedes that some of his successes may be due to suggestion, and seems to have developed a theory of psychosomatic disease of the soul; but he considers that cure by suggestion is rarer in his own than in orthodox treatment and that the latter may itself sometimes succeed only when helped by spirit intervention. Finally, he augments the advice to those who would follow in his steps – advice which he has spread throughout many books – with a good deal of common sense, lay psychology, and household medicine of variable soundness.

An examination paper on paranormal healing might well include such a question as 'Compare and contrast the methods, beliefs and vocabulary of C. Woodard and H. Edwards'; for in a few pages devoted to these two English contemporary healers we have met all those baffling similarities and differences which mark the history of this subject. But we have not yet done with contradictions and self-contradictions, as we shall see when we turn to the views on paranormal healing which are held by the historic churches.

# CHAPTER FOUR

# In the Eyes of the Church

THE typical citizen of our modern 'developed' countries may think of himself as a rational materialist. But in fact he is ruled by superstition rather than religion. He will half-credit almost anything he reads in his Sunday paper, including the astrology column and the hardly less dubious claims of some advertisements. But the views of a priest are to him suspect as tinged with mysticism.

This is surely an unjust dismissal, for even the most irreligious must recognize that (for example) the Catholic church has nearly two thousand years of experience of dealing with every facet of the human personality, including its 'paranormal' powers if they exist – and that, on the whole, it has been more sceptical of claims to possess such powers than have been the societies within which it has functioned. Authority and experience, in religion as in science, may bring their own danger of the closed mind. But the views on paranormal healing of those major churches, sects and denominations to which psychic therapy can never be more than one of many activities are worth our attention here, if only because they may colour the views on healing held by physicians and other expert witnesses who are also practising Christians.

It has already been explained that, through shortage both of space and of knowledge, we must confine ourselves primarily to the western Christian tradition – though it may be worth noting here that the modern orthodox Jew is enjoined to pray daily for his own and for others' health, but to consult a physician in time of need. Within that tradition, for both historical and statistical reasons, first consideration must be given to the Roman Catholic church. We left this at the time of the Reformation when (as in the third century) internal differences were damping its enthusiasm for healing. And subsequently we have done little more than note its difficulties in dealing with priests and laymen who took seriously and as applying to all time Christ's command to heal, and who believed they had a special talent for paranormal therapy.

'Christ the Healer is one of the eternal images or archetypes...' But this quotation is not from a religious dignitary but from Carl Jung; and it cannot be claimed that the Roman church has shown a more continued interest in paranormal healing than has any other or that it has succeeded in arriving at a consistent attitude towards it – or, for that matter, towards suffering in general. Although the Roman church has – particularly in the period of its active revival over the last century or more – pronounced 'infallibly' on a host of subjects both natural and (to use its own term) praeternatural, paranormal healing is not among them; and only in the most recent years has there been a growth of the belief that the healing power of the church may be an index of its spiritual liveliness.

Furthermore, the historic church has not extracted from the Gospels any formal rite or sacrament of healing. On the contrary, it has inclined at times towards the belief that all sickness may be God's will. Thus anointing with oil, originally curative in aim, was transformed during the Dark Ages into 'extreme unction' or a preparation for a (spiritually) good death. This was possibly so because it had proved so ineffective therapeutically: in the later Middle Ages, at any rate, those who recovered after its administration were treated as legally dead.

Similarly exorcism, in medieval times a panacea for all mental ills and one which could be administered by a lowly grade of clerk, became a rare rite requiring the permission of a bishop. (The original instructions from Christ to cast out devils were, of course, not to a special priesthood but to all believers.) Perhaps the only constant factor has been the belief of Catholics – and of all mainstream Christians – that the real merit of a physical cure is not in relief from suffering but in the evidence it gives of divine grace and in the means it supplies for the more important end of saving souls. This, it is claimed, was the attitude of Christ when in Matthew ix He told a man 'sick of the palsy' to take up his bed and walk *in order that* he might know that the Son of Man had the power to forgive sins.

Where the Roman church does help us is in supplying criteria for 'miracles' which, though suggested more than two centuries ago, remain meaningful to theologians, jurists and medical men. The word is commonly abused in such a way as to suggest any remarkable and apparently beneficial happening. But the church has set strict standards which must be satisfied before an event can even begin to be considered miraculous.

It must, for instance, be noteworthy and, by Catholic standards, edifying and reasonable. It is usually instantaneous, though some miracles developing over a period of time have been accepted: it occurs in answer to prayer, though not necessarily the prayer of the person chiefly concerned: and – where this is relevant – it must be persistent in its effects. Finally, it cannot be accepted *as* a miracle until there is an overwhelming weight of evidence that the event did in fact occur and that any natural explanation is supremely unlikely.

By such high standards many of the legendary feats attributed to the saints must be ruled out. For instance, the ability to change one's height at will, attributed to ancient mystics as well as to the celebrated nineteenth century medium Daniel Home, would only be deemed miraculous if it served a useful and holy purpose. And in our own field the attitude of the church reminds us of the need to differentiate between the faith cure and the miracle cure proper.

One Roman Catholic authority, for instance, concedes that the former may occur frequently, perhaps in answer to private prayer, and with that dismisses it. He follows Pope Benedict XIV's definition of the latter in stipulating that miracle cures should be impossible or very difficult to reproduce by known medical means: that the illness should not be declining, or likely to improve: that no medical treatment should have been given or that, if given, it should have proved ineffective some time before: that the cure should have been instantaneous and complete: that no natural crisis should have supervened: and finally that there should have been no relapse, at least for a period of years.

If the possibility of the miraculous is accepted at all, one can only criticize such criteria (as Dr Michael Balint has done) as being over-rigorous: an organization which takes decades or centuries to reach a verdict, too, may not be the best instrument to investigate phenomena whose assessment depends on living testimony. And in fact the Roman church demands little more of its members in this context than that they *should* accept that possibility: no believer is required to accept as a fact any particular post-apostolic miracle, therapeutic or otherwise, even when approved by the church, and a good deal of latitude is permitted even in relation to Christ's own miracles. As examples of phenomena which the church itself was not prepared to accept as miraculous, one may cite the cases of a nun who lived without food for thirty years and of a woman, known to be a religious fanatic, who about 1900 lost her speech and sight, ran a temperature of 108 deg. F. (42 deg. C.) and 'sweated blood' during a medical examination, but who, an hour after a communion service at which she had expressed her belief that she would be cured, had become well again. These well-witnessed events were dismissed by Roman Catholic priests and physicians alike as hysterical in origin.

Yet despite its scepticism the Roman church has, in the last century and a half, remained involved in paranormal healing in at least four ways. First, it has had to come to terms with its inherited traditions – for instance, the blessings of sore throats which take place on St Blaise's day, the 3 February. Secondly, the tests which a candidate for canonization must pass include the performance of 'indisputable' miracles before or after death: normally two in each class are required, and since the procedure was laid down in the seventeenth century at least half those accepted have been therapeutic even when the candidate had shown no general talent for healing. Thirdly, we have seen that some healers of less than saintly stature have practised within the church. And, finally, in recent times the Roman church has been inspired by the example of other denominations to set up 'healing centres' of intercessionary prayer such as the Priory of St John near Paris.

Among the more famous of modern healing saints are St John Vianney (the Curé d'Ars) with his cures of the deaf and blind, St Frances Cabrini, and Don (St John) Bosco. The latter remarkable personality of the nineteenth century has hundreds of paranormal cures to his credit. He preferred patients to be in a state of grace after confession and communion when they came to him, but admitted that in many cases a pill compounded of flour and water seemed to have curative powers almost as effective as that of the most pious prayer.

In this connexion it should be noted that in Catholic theology the power to work therapeutic or other miracles is not considered to be restricted to the saints or even the faithful but extends to all good men – and perhaps to less good ones also, for the church accepts that even the Devil may cure for his own ends. It pronounces, however, only on the activities of its own members; and even within that flock paranormal healing powers are regarded solely as evidence for sanctity and not as synonymous with it. Many canonized saints have themselves led lives wracked with pain.

Popular attention – at least outside the Roman church – has, however, tended to focus less on individual Catholic healers and their relics than on the shrines, springs and the like discovered as a result of revelations to otherwise unremarkable persons. In the last century or so there has been a typical pattern to these events: in unattractive surroundings, such as a municipal rubbish-tip, the Virgin Mary appears to an adolescent girl who has led an irreproachable life but who is not particularly intelligent or mentally stable and announces that benefits will accrue – in their future if not their present life – to those who pray to her at that site. Cures are claimed; and what follows leads to a soul-searching which spreads out, with immense care, from the parish priest and physician to curias and specialized medical groups. The person to whom the vision was granted may retire from the world and even become a canonized saint, but rarely displays healing powers.

The search for truth in such matters is not helped by the fact that the possession of a healing shrine becomes a national and regional status symbol: tourist and medical vested interests also soon become involved. But popular healing shrines supported by varying degrees of church approval currently include La Salette in France, Knock in Ireland, Loreto and Pompeii in Italy, Beauraing in Belgium, Fatima in Portugal and one at Quebec in Canada which dates from the seventeenth century: there are also hundreds of minor Roman churches in which an altar surrounded by crutches, plaster casts and votive plaques can be seen, and hundreds more are to be found in the Greek Orthodox church. To an outsider, however, the exemplar is the small town in the Pyrenees which, at 12.30 p.m. on 11 February 1858, was set on the road to international fame by the visions of an illiterate and asthmatic fourteen-year-old girl, the later-canonized Bernadette Soubirous.

Lourdes has attracted a vast bibliography, and I greatly regret that, after I had planned an inquiry of my own there, I was unable for personal reasons to carry it out. But the essential facts are these.

Even before St Bernadette's visions had come under official investigation (and the Virgin promised no specific therapeutic or even temporal benefits to those who worshipped at her shrine or bathed in the spring which marks the site of her appearance at the cave of Massabielle), local sufferers began to visit the spot and physicians were becoming impressed by its powers. Over the next thirty years cures were claimed at irregular intervals but at an average of two a week; but it is now admitted by Catholic authorities that the standards of examination at first applied were lax and that the claims were not uninfluenced by the propagandist mood of the church at that time.

In particular, the Catholic press sensationalized many purported cures. In return sceptics such as Emile Zola, who visited Lourdes in the early 1890s, replied with still more superficial 'exposures'. This era of highly-coloured reports (only the Society for Psychical Research, with a non-committal paper published in 1894, tried to preserve a balance) perhaps reached its peak with the *Journey to Lourdes* of Alexis Carrel, a Nobel prizewinner in medicine who is believed to have written the dramatic account of a change of opinion brought about by a visit to the shrine in 1903. Subsequently Dr Carrel co-operated with an English physician, Dr Howard Somervell, in approving a number of 'miraculous' cures.

Since then the emotional temperature at Lourdes has fallen so far as medical controversies are concerned. An organization which dates back to 1882 and which is staffed by Roman Catholic physicians but welcomes investigations by others examines the thousands of claims of miraculous cures made every year: of these claims about fifty pass a first screening, six a second one and perhaps a single case is left at the end to be accepted as a probable miracle. As its version of the Catholic standards for the examination of miraculous events, the *Bureau des Constatations Medicales* stipulates (and here I somewhat simplify the criteria) that for a cure to be accepted the sufferer's medical state must have been certified by expert diagnosis before the visit, that the morbid condition concerned must be organic and have been regarded as incurable or at best as amenable only to very lengthy treatment, but that in fact an immediate recovery, which persisted at the time of the examination, took place when the shrine was visited.

According to Roman Catholic physicians a proportion of cures satisfy even these very strict conditions, and in some cases as many as seventy medical witnesses have testified to the miraculous quality of a recovery. Dr D. J. West, however, took eleven recent 'established' Lourdes miracles and found flaws in the evidence for every one. He also raised general objections: for instance, he found weaknesses in both the documentary and clinical facilities of the Bureau and remarked on the lack of a single instance of a miracle similar to that of St Winefride, the few dubious examples of cures of malignant tumours but the many cases of inadequately-established tuberculosis, and the preponderance of elderly spinsters among the patients to receive benefit. It is also striking that, although the annual attendance rate at Lourdes has rocketed from a few thousand to several million, the number of attested cures each year remains fairly constant.

Furthermore, despite the fact that Lourdes is one of the few places where religion and medicine work in concert, we are still disappointed in our search for controlled studies. 'In the absence of a research team investigating whole groups of pilgrims . . .' Dr West points out, '. . . one cannot be sure that a special curative factor exists, much less find out how it works.' In fact, although the shrine remains a centre for considering such curious cases as that of the paralysed French atheist who challenged God to cure the blind boy next to him and who found that he was himself cured and the boy was not, the accent has moved away from the dramatic physical cures which appealed (or appalled) in the last century and towards the claim that the Virgin confers *some* benefit on all who worship there.

Roman Catholics, indeed, now assert that the majority of the faithful who visit Lourdes annually do not expect physical benefits so much as spiritual uplift and that those who *are* healed are frequently surprised at the fact. Certainly acute observers, including many non-Catholics and even non-Christians, have remarked that the place seems impregnated with a quality of well-being and that very few leave it without some psychological improvement. Other curious facts are that no case of infection has ever been traced to the baths of holy water (of which the hygienic standards are somewhat alarming), and that many of the cures are less than complete, the imperfection being supposedly left as a reminder of divine intervention.

Modern critics of Lourdes tend to be less frequently materialists than the campaigners for Spiritualism who make a platform-point of the fact that, in its history of more than a century, only forty-nine 'miracle' cures deriving from treatment at, or associated with, Lourdes have been sanctioned. Even the total acceptable on medical but not on theological grounds runs to only a thousand or so in all, whereas the Spiritualist healers claim thousands *every year*. In particular Harry Edwards formerly took the view that the contrast was overwhelmingly in his favour, though he has more recently recognized that the Lourdes investigations are more intensive than any which he or his colleagues have applied to themselves.

But in view of the facts that the successes which are fully accepted by the church (and which are still queried by Dr West) are estimated at perhaps one in two million, and that even marked physical improvements as a whole run at only about two per cent, it does not appear that expectations of health alone would justify a pilgrimage to Lourdes. The significance of the shrine would seem to be religious rather than medical; and indeed the sick are now discouraged from visiting Lourdes, or any similar establishment, until all conventional treatments have failed. Perhaps it should be stressed that a belief that the shrine has any efficacy at all is by no means an article of faith for Catholics.

At the other extreme from the outward solidarity of the Roman Catholic church is the whole group of dissenting sects who remain more closely linked with orthodox Christianity than do the 'Christian Scientists', Spiritualists and individual evangelists considered in the previous chapter. These nonconformists form a spectrum of their own, and range from the extreme 'left' of the pentecostal or revivalist groups (such as that of Pastor Jeffreys) which hold out healing as a prize for conversion to their peculiar form of Christianity to the Methodists who stand to the 'right' of many evangelical adherents to the Church of England.

We have already seen that from the Reformation onwards certain dissenters – those in the tradition of Martin Luther rather than of John Calvin – adopted a belief in the therapeutic powers of the Christian faith. This belief was, for instance, characteristic of the Moravians and Waldenses of the sixteenth century, of the Baptists and Quakers of the seventeenth (George Fox being a healer of repute, though one who seems to have needed to be specifically 'moved of the Lord' to this activity), of the Wesleyans and a host of minor groups still surviving in the United States in the eighteenth, and in the nineteenth of such ill-assorted sects as the Irvingites and the 'Peculiar People'. The Mormons too have curious devices of their own, such as 'holy handkerchiefs' and a healing tradition which dates back to Joseph Smith – who believed that faith was all, but who failed to control an epidemic of cholera within his flock. In all these persuasions there was a general tendency to abandon ritual (though some use was still made of anointing) and to lay increased stress on prayer and the laying on of hands.

In modern times certain of these free churches have shown almost no interest in spiritual healing, while for others it has become an important part of their pastoral activity. As examples of the latter we may select the 'Four-Square Gospellers' – essentially a healing mission inspired by Miss McPherson's 'New Thought' – the Mormons, the 'Moral Rearmament' movement and the Quakers, whose Friends' Spiritual Healing Fellowship maintains a rest home in Surrey and claims a high success-rate.

Typical of the groups which, at least in Britain, have shown less enthusiasm for healing are the Baptists, Congregationalists, Presbyterians and perhaps Unitarians. Some of these, however, are therapeutically active in the United States, and in Britain have individual members committed to spiritual healing such as the Congregationalist (and Spiritualist) Rev. Alex Holmes. The English Presbyterians, too, have in the Rev. Dr George May a spiritual healer and in the Rev. Harry Hutchison an advocate of more conventional methods, and a Presbyterian physician practises healing in Wales.

In Scotland, the home of Presbyterianism, interest was kindled by the Rev. J. Cameron Peddie: he felt a call to practise a ministry of healing, but found no power to do so until the age of fifty-five and after five years of prayer. From these later years he has described, in addition to numerous cures, such mystical experiences as a vision of the stigmata and the sweating of perfumed oil. Mr Peddie believed that his healing methods were invariably effective for rheumatic disease: in cases of cancer he claimed that he could almost always alleviate pain (though sometimes only by repeated services), often secure a remission, and occasionally effect a complete cure: he also held that God warned him when he might be doing harm. He believed in a regular healing hour and in absent treatment, and in the course of 'healing' his wife ('there was little wrong with her,' he admitted, 'but a service always had a tonic effect ...') conducted an experiment in which it appeared that her higher blood pressure was partially transferred to himself. He also accidentally discovered that he could help domestic animals.

Polls taken in the United States suggest that there one nonconformist minister in four has had some experience of spiritual cures. In continental Europe too, and particularly in the Germanic countries, the reformed churches have in the last hundred years or so shown a growing interest in healing. Individuals of note here include the Swiss healer Dorothy Trudel, Pastor Johann Blumhardt of Stuttgart (who purchased an entire spa and ran it as a faith-healing centre about 1850) and Fr John of Kronstadt who carried the tradition into the Russian Orthodox world.

Ministers of these churches have, however, generally admitted to gaining more inspiration from the Anglican tradition than from nonconformist development.

A denomination which calls for special note is that of the Methodists, a mid-stream persuasion critical equally of Catholic sacramentalism and evangelical emotionalism. Their founder, John Wesley, was an (intermittently) healing preacher whose methods have been compared to convulsive therapy by a psychiatrist who considers that his sermons provided 'physiological as well as psychological aids'. Wesley is also credited with the cure by faith of his horse. He wrote that 'the love of God ... is the sovereign remedy of all miseries ... the most powerful of all the means of health and long life': he also believed, in spite of his faith in 'the proper use of the electrical machine', that all disease was due to demonism. Members of this movement have always prayed that their ministers be granted curative powers and have perhaps generally shown the degree of interest in paranormal healing now exemplified by Lord Soper. Despite the energetic work of the American 'New Life' movement under Dr Albert Day, however, the current international as well as British importance of Methodism in the sphere of healing is largely attributable to the work of Dr Leslie Weatherhead, the preacher, writer and (despite his mistrust of the press) publicist.

Dr Weatherhead does not necessarily represent his church, and certainly does not claim to be an infallible spokesman. But even as a private individual his views are of considerable interest for three reasons. First, he is a lay psychologist whose experience dates back to World War I: secondly, he has written several important, thoughtful and well-researched books on the relation between religious belief and mental and bodily health: and, thirdly, his views are typical of a school of protestant theologians such as the Swiss Pastor Bernard Martin. The latter, incidentally, cites an interesting case of pyelitis in which both a prayer group and the absent patient were simultaneously inspired to try a remedy which proved successful though unusual in their circle, anointing with oil.

In many of Dr Weatherhead's books one is struck by what appears to be a conflict between his naturally cautious, inquiring and scientific attitude and his commitment to his faith. (The author himself distinguishes between the 'theological' faith which can be embodied in a creed and a less precise 'trustful expectancy' which may still lead to paranormal experiences and which must itself be differentiated from mere suggestibility.) Like many theorists on this subject he dismisses all rival schools of healing, from Lourdes to Spiritualism, as ineffective, dangerous or unacceptable on doctrinal grounds. His own views, however, lead him to the theologically-questionable conclusion that there are *laws* of prayer and that it is useless, for example, to pray for protection from physical danger. It is hard to equate this opinion with Christ's promise that believers would be safe from poisons and serpents; and the distinction is in fact dismissed by a fellow Methodist, the Rev. Bertram Woods.

Concerning faith healers in general, Dr Weatherhead says that 'After much consideration, it is my view that there are certain people with strange psychic gifts who ... have brought healing to some. The power of suggestion plays a part in such cures, but does not wholly explain them. The gift is often quite separated from any profession of Christianity.' Such healers, whom Dr Weatherhead occasionally refers to as 'eccentric', should, he feels, practise only under the guidance of a 'priest or minister'; and he asserts that their methods 'should be distinguished from the one which the Church sanctioned'. Elsewhere he dismisses the power to cure as a 'freak endowment' which should be contrasted with the disciplined methods of the church.

At other times, however, Dr Weatherhead appears to diminish his concept of Christianity to a status little higher than that of a primitive psychiatry. For example, he makes the point that Christ's deliberate acts of healing seem to have followed inquiries into the needs of the particular sufferer and were hence very different from the mass-production methods used by popular faith healers. He also states that not only would it be useless for him to attempt by paranormal means so minor a feat as the removal of a bone stuck in a throat but also that Christ Himself would not, and perhaps *could* not, have done so. Where Dr Weatherhead differs from both Catholic and evangelical tradition is implicit in such a statement as 'It is impossible for the modern man to believe ... that Christ could restore in a moment the health of a man whose head had been severed from the neck.' Whether or not Christ did perform such a miracle is immaterial to those believers who would not accept such a limitation on His powers. Indeed, extreme 'Christian Scientist' and Spiritualist healers might not so limit their own.

Dr Weatherhead's theology is certainly not completely satisfying, and indeed many of his free church colleagues seem to mistrust the attempts at systematization inherent in his approach to a philosophy of healing. Can we, then, take more guidance from the practical side of his experience, and in particular his work at the City Temple, London?

Since 1936 Dr Weatherhead has made this church – with two interruptions – a centre for an attack on human problems, his weapons there being psychiatric as well as specifically Christian. Curiously enough, his description of his methods forms one of the less satisfactory features of his books, but it appears that two main and quite different courses are followed. The first is the examination and counselling of patients by a panel of seven or eight medically-qualified Christians with psychiatric experience. the second is the 'lifting up to Christ' of sufferers (who are not necessarily present) by mentioning their names in the course of a service. There may also be sessions of private witness and specialized prayer with the sick to 'clear the path for God'.

What has been the result of this whole range of activities? Dr Weatherhead makes passing references to the healing of sceptics and of sufferers from 'incurable' diseases, and states that 'a significant proportion' of those to whom he ministered between 1940 and 1965 took 'a turn for the better'. But once again we are given no comparative statistics, and in the course of a long book devoted to the subject of healing Dr Weatherhead cites only one detailed case history, that of a child who recovered from severe nephritis. His own faith is undiminished and he claims that, whilst his methods constitute no cure-all and could be vastly improved in efficacy by some form of combined scientific and theological research, they have shown results such as would lead to a new drug being used and accepted as a curative agent despite failures. Until further figures are published, however, it is difficult to accept even this limited claim, and one is more impressed by Bertram Woods' admission that 'the proportion of healing [by the methods used in the nonconformist churches] is small – very small'.

A corporate Methodist interest in healing has been manifested in the last twenty years by that denomination's Society for Medical and Pastoral Practice. In the Church of England – which, for all its range of internal differences, sets the tone for numerous overseas communions – a revival of interest came at the start of the present century with the activities of James Moore Hickson. Hickson was, and remained, a layman; but he was also a pious church-man. Hence, when he discovered that he had the gift of healing (which he exercised through laying on of hands and directed, for the most part, to treating minor aches and pains) he decided to use it to the greater glory of God. He refused to practise unless an Anglican priest was present, and hoped that his work would lead to a revival of interest in healing within the church itself.

Hickson – who later, together with his disciple H. A. Madge, became a convinced believer in diabolical possession and claimed many instances of successful exorcism – travelled widely and was fairly well known both before and after the First World War. He has left two main memorials – the Divine Healing Mission, which remains active within his church, and a Home of Healing at Crowhurst in Sussex which was founded in 1928 by one of his clerical advisers, the Rev. Howard Cobb. The treatment at this centre, which accepts some two hundred patients yearly, resembles that at the City Temple in that it is largely psychiatric in nature and is not directed towards 'miracle' cures. It is not easy, in fact, to see the difference between such an establishment and any other well-conducted retreat for recovery after mental illness such as the 'Christian rest homes' (which are not under clerical direction) of Protestant Europe.

Another approach within the Anglican church derives from the Rev. John Maillard who, though opposed to Spiritualism, believed that he was inspired through the communion of saints by his deceased relatives and who conducted prayer sessions by telephone. Maillard organized the dedication of a Brighton church to divine healing and later, in 1937, founded Milton Abbey, Dorset, as the headquarters of an order devoted to such work. This establishment broke up as a result of internal dissensions about the respective rights of its medical and clerical advisers, not without adverse comments from those who regarded it as a home for wealthy hypochondriacs in search of priestly father-figures. A successor was founded at Oke-hampton, Devon, however, and the Rev. James Wilson continues to have a critical faith in its work. A cross-breeding between Milton Abbey and the Hickson school produced, in 1949, the London Healing Mission.

Of the corporate, rather than primarily individual, cura-tive movements within the Church of England the senior is the Guild of Health, which was established in 1905 by three priests including the Rev. Conrad Noel. At about the same time a somewhat similar body, the Emmanuel Movement, was set up despite considerable opposition within the episcopal church of the United States: one of its two clerical founders had received some training in psychology at Oxford and the movement was in its turn to influence the British school. Its members appear to have been dispersed during the last war, but its work continues under different names such as that of the Fellowship of St Luke which was founded by an English-born episcopa-lian in 1947. The links between religion and therapy are in general closer in the USA, with its church-sponsored hospitals, than in Britain.

The aim of the Guild of Health was to 'arouse the whole protestant church to the place [in it] of spiritual healing'. Its methods include anointing and the laying on of hands after the religious preparation of the sufferer, prayer groups, and a form of psychotherapy. It undertakes re-search and attempts to reach understanding with members of the medical profession: it also welcomes co-operation with protestants of all denominations.

Ten years younger is the Guild of St Raphael, which takes a more exclusive and high-church line and places greater emphasis on the sacraments and on formalized rules of prayer. This differs from its predecessor in that it leaves psychiatry to psychiatrists, and assumes a more 'catholic' attitude in not necessarily expecting physical results but being content to 'leave the answer to God'. Its particular platform is the rescue of the sacrament of holy (*not* extreme) unction from its comparative disuse by protestants and its steady debasement by Roman Catholics – which had continued since the Council of Trent in the middle of the sixteenth century – into a preparation for death.

In the same category are the nursing homes – which have both medical and clerical approval – which were established after 1929 by Dorothy Kerin, an Anglican mystic who was cured of phthisis, tuberculous peritonitis, meningitis and blindness through her faith in God in 1912, and whose experience included visions of the Virgin and the discovery of a holy spring. Miss Kerin, whose work culminated in the building of an undenominational church dedicated to Christ the Healer at Burrswood, Kent, is said to have performed a number of miracle cures. The diseases concerned seem mostly to have been psychogenic and the sufferers women, though the distinguished physicist George Searle claimed to have been cured simply as a result of reading Miss Kerin's book and her work so impressed the then Archbishop of Canterbury (and also Lord Horder) that a service of thanksgiving was held in 1961 and filled St Paul's Cathedral.

There are also a number of ecumenical, but primarily Anglican, bodies which should be mentioned in this context. One is the Churches' Council of Healing, established in 1944 and currently headed by the Archbishop of Canterbury. The Churches' Fellowship for Psychical Study, which has a healing subcommittee, is a minority group established in 1954 by two priests and a layman: it now numbers a dozen Anglican prelates as well as Dr Weatherhead among its vice-presidents, but is too sympathetic to

Spiritualism to be wholly approved by the major churches. It practises synchronized prayer and absent healing, and also undertakes research: at its foundation, for instance, its members believed that they could gather convincing evidence for the occurrence of paranormal healing within six months . . .

Finally, there are within the established churches in Britain a number of more localized groups with a special interest in paranormal healing. Perhaps the most 'respectable' of these is the Iona Community, whose main sponsor is the (Presbyterian) Church of Scotland: its founder and director, the Rev. Dr George MacLeod – later moderator of the general assembly of the Church of Scotland – was inspired by the blind Anglican healer Dr Godfrey Mowatt to set up a healing ministry on the island using the techniques of synchronized prayer and laying on of hands. It is also characteristic of the Church of England that it has always given a good deal of freedom to individual enthusiasts such as the Ven. A. F. Sharp, who practised psychic healing during his ministry of some sixty years. Currently Canon J. D. Pearce-Higgins, Vice-Provost of Southwark, is perhaps the leading spokesman for the view that the Church of England should lay far more stress in its liturgy on spiritual healing. But though figures are harder to come by in Britain than in the USA there must be many hundreds of Anglican priests who conduct regular services of intercession for the sick, some without great enthusiasm but under pressure from their congregations. And almost every clergyman or church worker knows of at least one case of a remarkable cure – such as that of Sir Francis Chichester's cancer – coinciding with the administration of a sacrament or with intense private prayer.

These clergy may differ both in theology and in their claims for success – which range from 'virtually all cases' to 'very rare'. But they can be divided into two main groups, which perhaps represent fundamentally different views on the nature of prayer itself: some ask God to heal *if it be His will*, while others confidently instruct the sufferer to be well. Neither, however, can be regarded as expressing the official views of the church; and these are indeed difficult to determine when considering a body whose own bishops openly disagree as to the value of paranormal healing.

A middle-of-the-road Anglican view might be that the question of credence in the Gospel miracles can be left to the individual, that a belief in post-apostolic miracles is regarded as somewhat high church, and that the evangelical fervour of the mass healing meeting is to be eschewed. (Many non-conformists share this view of healing 'rallies', regarding them as in some way dangerous: the mistrust, however, appears to be more on aesthetic and psychological than on theological grounds.) The exorcism of persons as opposed to places, which formed part of the baptismal service before the Reformation, is in some sectors of the church almost a routine matter and in others virtually unknown: unction was, in the prayer book of 1719, restored to the status it held in the early church but has since either been neglected once more or (despite archiepiscopal recommendations made some thirty-five years ago) been left mainly to sacramentalists: and according to some Anglicans there is no need for a special rite of laying on of hands since this is implicit in the normal act of blessing.

In an attempt to introduce a degree of uniformity of belief and usage, and on the incentive of the Hickson and Noel movements, an Archbishop of Canterbury set up an investigation of the problems of paranormal healing as long ago as 1908. Very little came of this, however, or of its successor, the Lambeth Committee of 1920 on the Healing Ministry in the Christian Church, whose main conclusion was that healing missions were to be discouraged since those who attended them were insufficiently prepared spiritually. Despite the fact that Archbishops William Temple and Gordon Lang were both interested in the subject and had established various councils to investigate it, the matter was generally dropped again until the late 1940s. But in 1953 the then Archbishops of Canterbury and York set up a commission of twenty-eight, mainly clerics and physicians, 'to consider the theological, medical, psychological and pastoral aspects of divine healing with a view to providing within two or three years a report designed to guide the church to clearer understanding of the subject'.

Many of the members seem to have shown no previous interest in the subject, and in addition leading prelates known to be convinced of the effectiveness of divine healing such as Canon Roger Lloyd were not on the body. Furthermore, its structure was somewhat unwieldy and all its members were present at only seventeen meetings. Evidence was gathered from no more than twelve outsiders, including Dr Weatherhead, Dr Woodard, Harry Edwards, three or four other healers mentioned earlier, and myself. The 'two or three years' became five. But eventually, in 1958, a report on *The Church's Ministry of Healing* appeared.

This consisted of only eighty-four small pages of guarded and heavily qualified prose. It was received with very little enthusiasm, which was perhaps not surprising since the panel began by assuming that it was not competent to assess evidence on the efficacy of paranormal healing and went on to give advice of interest mainly to parish priests. There were, however, minority signatories such as the Spiritualist priest the Rev. Maurice Elliot.

In summary, the tone of the report was apologetic in that it accepted the retreat of faith before science and of authority before public opinion. Theologically it appeared

negative where not self-contradictory. And – most remarkably – on its last page it referred to the 'unusual gift of
healing which some persons seem to have' without having
previously made any detailed discussion of these persons
or their claims.

But the enterprise *did* focus considerable public attention on paranormal healing. Furthermore, despite the massive representation of physicians on the parent body, the
archbishops' commission had felt itself as unable to deal
with the medical as with the evidential issues involved and
on the former score had sought the co-operation of the
British Medical Association: this in fact had brought out,
in 1956 or two years before the main report, its own findings on healing. This document accepted 'miracle' cures
as theoretically possible but saw no evidence for them: it
also avoided cardinal issues by *assuming* that all paranormal therapy depended on suggestion. It could, however,
be regarded as an advance on a similar report issued nearly
fifty years previously which had been distinctly hostile to
religious healing, and a later BMA statement conceded
that recoveries took place through spiritual healing which
could not be medically explained.

Meanwhile, Harry Edwards had something of a field-
day. His examination by the archbishops' commission
early in 1955, which roughly coincided with a rather
stormy television appearance, had led him to suspect that
both the commission itself and the medical panel would
regard his views unsympathetically. He claimed that after
submitting seventy 'case histories' he had provided the
medical experts with more than the six instances of successful cures for which he had been asked; and in the absence of any reply to his subsequent complaints he would
appear to have a case to answer in claiming that there
were elements of negligence in the investigation of them.
It was firmly stated by Mr Edwards that the British Medi-

cal Association report contained inaccuracies concerning these cases; the archbishops' commission made no mention of them at all.

Perhaps neither the medical nor the clerical professions emerged with enhanced stature from these inquiries. But their representatives were not the only puzzled men; for looking back over this summary of a literature which would itself fill a bookcase it is difficult to believe that any one Christian church – and still less the churches as a whole – has a more coherent view of the nature and validity of faith healing than have the independents and heretics.

Possibly there is today a consensus that God wants men to be healthy: that prayer and other religious techniques can help bring this about: that paranormal cures must be attempted with love and are at best only a means to the end of salvation (and here the Spiritualist who heals for healing's own sake is perhaps closer to the orthodox physician than is the Christian healer): that medical co-operation is always desirable: and – above all – that failure is frequent. But beyond this we find only the familiar noise of many voices, but little harmony.

# CHAPTER FIVE

## Many Questions, Some Answers

THE first time I saw Harry Edwards in action was on 10 March 1951 at a demonstration of 'spirit healing' held at the Kingsway Hall, London. The majority of his patients on that day appeared to be suffering from crippling disorders of bone and muscle; and as one after another left the platform many seemed to have achieved, at a touch from the healer, the free and painless movements of limbs which – on their own testimony at least – had for years resisted orthodox medical treatment. But even in this emotionally charged atmosphere it struck me that Mr Edwards was, perhaps unconsciously, 'editing' his patients' testimony and suggesting to them appropriate responses.

Later, as I was leaving the hall, I saw a woman walking with the help of two sticks on which she leaned heavily. At other times this would have been a commonplace, though pathetic, sight. But I suddenly realized that this was the same woman who, an hour or so earlier, had walked down the steps from the platform to the auditorium without the aid of her sticks, glowing with joy at her 'cure' and at taking her first unaided paces for several years.

This was, of course, a single observation and of no more evidential value than those cases of 'successful' faith cures which from time to time flare up in the sensational weekend press and which fill the psychic weeklies. But it set me thinking once more of the great difficulties I was likely to meet in surveying this field of faith healing. Would I be able to achieve even the degree of certainty called for in a court of law – a degree which in turn is less than that on which scientific and even medical theories become universally accepted? For every phenomenon there seemed a counter-phenomenon: for every explanation, an alternative explanation.

I originally intended to call this chapter of discussion 'Questions and Answers', but I have had to modify that title. Most of the evidence which I have discussed earlier is diffuse, coloured and suspect: most of the conclusions which might be drawn from it are challengeable: and we can reach no firm conclusions. But at this stage in our search for truth a useful purpose may be served simply by asking what appear to be the right questions.

I have already stressed that I believe in the importance as well as the complexity of this subject. The outcome of the 'Loch Ness monster' controversy, for instance, is unlikely fundamentally to alter our outlook on the world. But if – not one perhaps but ten or a hundred – examples were found of diseases being cured by some mechanism which could not be explained other than by the intervention of intelligences operating from outside our ordinary world, then even the practical benefits would be as nothing to the scientific, religious and philosophical implications.

For this reason alone the most scrupulous standards of examination must be brought to bear on the phenomena of faith healing, and fortunately we have a yardstick which has served for six centuries. This is 'Ockham's razor', which states that we must not increase our postulates until we are compelled to do so. With this razor in hand we must examine the claims of faith healers of all persuasions, accepting nothing without the most careful examination.

On this basis let us review the material to hand, and first consider the nature of the healers themselves. At the outset of my inquiry I hoped that I might discover some common factor in the personalities of the various healers, their methods or the ways in which they regarded themselves and were regarded by their contemporaries: certainly I could look for little more from testimony in which there is not a single detailed case-history, where 'some', 'most', or 'all' do duty for statistics, and where there is only the most primitive attempt at cross-examination or controlled study. But in fact, in the twenty centuries which separate the first Christian apostle from the latest Spiritualist miracle-worker, we find no 'typical' faith healer but only an apparently random group of men and women.

Faith-inspired early Christians, ignorant peasants, flamboyant showmen, puzzled soldiers, distressed priests, self-appointed mystics and hard-headed businessmen: those who developed their powers late and those who lost them soon and those who kept them for most of their lives: the few who can be justly accused of charlatanism and the vast majority who made no more than a humble income from their powers: all these seem to have had, in their age, the ability to convince their contemporaries that maladies could be cured by a word, a touch, a prayer. Even the explanations which they have given of their powers seem to recur with no significant elaboration through the generations and the centuries.

There is indeed a quality in this varied mass of material which persuades one that it must be given serious attention; at the lowest estimate we are dealing, not with a fundamentally trivial isolated mystery such as those of the *Marie Celeste*, the Devils of Loudun or the Talking Mongoose of Man, but with conviction on the grandest scale. Not tarantism nor flying saucers, not alchemy nor witch-hunting, not palmistry nor phrenology nor even astrology itself can have made so many converts over so long a period as has the belief that some form of mental or spiritual activity can induce major improvements in human health. Furthermore, from the pre-Christian era through the ages of the Stroker and the Zouave and the nineteenth-century Theosophists and on to the present day, we seem to be dealing with the same type of phenomena or at most with two or three closely related types: for instance, there are similarities such as the report of a tingling sensation being shared by healer and healed to be found in the testimony of those of very different persuasions. There is surely *some* insight into the human personality to be gained here.

Another significant point emerges when we consider the passive side of the healing relationship, the nature of the sufferer and of the diseases treated. Detailed analysis is of course impossible, since even for the healers of the last century we lack not only clinical records but even a meaningful terminology. Nor am I sure that there is evidence for the view that the unorthodox healer is substantially successful only with the insecure middle-aged, with adolescents and with highly 'suggestible' subjects, though modern healers appear to have a disproportionate number of female patients. But it is clear that the faith healers' record is far more impressive with some types of ailment than with others, and a consideration of the claims of certain individual healers to specialize in one or other disease would only obscure this issue.

Whether in the seventeenth or the twentieth century, for instance, cases of 'trauma' healing – for example, the restoration of sight to eyes damaged by gunshot wounds – are hard to find, and there is no parallel in history to the legendary act of St Beuno which we took as an archetype of the indisputable miracle. Cures of infectious diseases, ill-defined in the past as plagues and poxes, *are* mentioned, but not with a frequency proportionate to their incidence in the seventeenth, eighteenth and early nineteenth centuries; and perhaps the same comment applies to malignant growths. Deformities feature in an unusually ill-defined group even today. But there are claims by the thousand for cures of certain forms of blindness and deafness, for lameness and many types of muscular and bone diseases, for dermatitis and above all for the distempers classified in their time as fits and agues, palsies and paralyses and epilepsies.

This high proportion of diseases which can broadly be termed 'functional' (perhaps an unsatisfactory term, but one now regarded as more appropriate than 'hysterical') as opposed to 'organic' suggests that the mechanism whose power was recognized by the authors of the *Malleus Maleficarum* when they attempted to distinguish between subjective and objective causation nearly five hundred years ago plays at least a role – and perhaps an important role – in the faith healer's successes. But before we move on to this topic we must ask one more question. Has any school of healers proved so much more successful than the others that it warrants our special attention here?

There has been no shortage of *names* attached to the purported power behind paranormal healing. Paracelsus and van Helmont spoke of the 'mumia' or 'magnum magnate', Mesmer of 'animal magnetism', and nineteenth-century investigators such as the millionaire inventor Reichenbach of 'odyle', 'orgone', 'X-forces' or 'Q-powers'. A passing knowledge of relativity, quantum mechanics and the principle of indeterminancy have led certain modern enthusiasts towards resounding but misleading parallels with the established phenomena of physics: others, ranging from Roman Catholic saints through the leaders of the Reformation to Mrs Eddy, have put their trust in God's will and others again in the intervention of departed spirits: and yet another group has been content with the idea of a focus of spiritual energy which may inhere in a place such as Lourdes as well as in a person. Equally diverse are the practices of various healers and their schools. In an interesting table the Rev. Bertram Woods compares thirty-three such in terms of twenty-seven characteristics, and finds a different permutation of faith or usage for nearly all.

But behind these obscurities of language and differences in method we can distinguish the three main outlooks of the materialist, the Christian (or at least monotheist) and the Spiritualist. Since Mesmer's time less and less has been heard from the first of these groups: an immensely expanded knowledge of the measurable forces of the universe has left reduced room for the concept of some vaguely disseminated healing power, and in any case the relief of a multitude of different symptoms would seem to involve some form of intelligence in the therapeutic agent. The controversy today, at least in the west, is hence primarily between the Christians and the Spiritualists. The former, for all their considerable sectarian differences, believe healing to derive fairly directly from the special acts of mercy of a single supreme power; the latter claim that the gift of healing is bestowed almost automatically by numerous spirits of the dead.

Since we have not yet established the validity of paranormal healing it would seem premature to attempt a comparison of the results of these two schools. It would be even less relevant here to discuss their articles of belief. But perhaps we may depart from a strict sequence when a conclusion seems to force itself upon us, as I think one now does.

This is, that there is no evidence that Christian healings, whether in the form of miracles at Catholic shrines, the activities of revivalist preachers or the work of the Quakers, are any more efficacious than those of the Spiritualists. Fr Thurston, for instance, complained of 'Christian Science' that 'the trouble is that many other practitioners who repudiate every one of Mrs Eddy's distinctive principles ... have accomplished equally remarkable and still better-attested cures'; but he did not go on to point out that the same was true of Lourdes. All that seems clear is that the responsible churches apply more critical standards to themselves than do the Spiritualists – and that their apparent successes are correspondingly fewer.

This fact has been recognized by several of the more thoughtful Christian apologists, some of whom have however suggested – without presenting evidence – that their own cures are superior in moral or medical quality to those of the Spiritualists and Pentecostals. Some, including the Rev. F. L. Wyman (an Anglican antagonist of Spiritualism who seems to believe that Christians should consult a priest before they go to a physician) have claimed that there are two separate forms of healing, a prayerful, Christian or 'divine' type and a more mechanistic one. The surgeon wife of the physicist Sir William Barrett suggested that there were three, and a follower of Harry Edwards named four – faith healing, spiritual healing, magnetic healing and psychic healing. But, grasping Ockham's razor, we should surely reject this multiplication of postulates.

Dr Rendle Short concluded 'there must be some common foundation for all these phenomena of healing' (assuming, that is, that we accept them at all) 'not dependent ... on the doctrine preached or the ceremony gone through.' An American Presbyterian, Professor Wade Boggs, has also complained that the beliefs and practices of various healing schools 'differ ... radically, and contradict each other at so many vital points'. 'Sometimes,' Professor Boggs continues, 'these cures are attributed directly to the healing power of God. Again, the faith of the sick man, and of his friends, is said to play a part. Prayer is considered essential by many. Value is often attributed to such means as sacramental oil, or the laying on of hands.... The successes of Christian Science healers are said to result from their fierce denials of the reality of matter in general, and of sickness or pain in particular. Others attribute healing power to the guidance of spirits, others to the Virgin Mary, others to the relics of dead saints. . . . The theories behind these healing movements vary widely and in fact are often radically opposed to one another. Yet all of them alike can point to certain successful cures, and all of them alike have a high percentage of failures.'

Similar results, he could have added, have also apparently been achieved by those whose beliefs are rooted in Islam or Jewry. As Origen wrote more than 1,500 years ago, the curative power appeared to be 'within the reach of godless as well as honest folk. The power of curing diseases is no evidence of anything specially divine'.

Beyond this lie many further questions. Is the healing power – if it exists – sacerdotal, charismatic or innate in all men and women? Is the faith of the patient important? (Most healers would answer 'No' to this question, especially those who believe that they are successful with very young children, animals and plants.) How are failures to be explained, and how are they linked to the great 'failure' of death?

Such questions may or may not be confidently answered (if they are it is on doctrinal rather than evidential grounds) by the adherents of the various schools of healing; and the number and variety of their answers, like the wide range of their modes of practice, may or may not influence the sceptic to take further serious interest in the subject. But we have yet to establish that any healing power exists; and before we can do that we must eliminate the possibility that the type of phenomena of which examples have filled this book can be explained reasonably without using more than the accepted mechanistic ideas of science and medicine.

Several of these ideas are comprised in the term 'suggestion'. This is one frequently employed by lay sceptics, but its scope is still a matter for considerable discussion within the medical profession. (It is relevant to 'brain washing', for instance, as described by Dr William Sargant in his book *Battle for the Mind*.) More has been discovered in recent years, however, than has passed into general knowledge; and there are some interesting facts to be presented concerning its manifestations.

It is part of the lore of medicine, and a part which was never lost sight of in the East, that psychological causes can have physical effects – some of them instantaneous and others curiously delayed. Such obvious phenomena as laughing and crying, blushing with shame, trembling with fear, vomiting with disgust, fainting with shock and similar emotionally determined reactions are common experience; and even if no Victorian young lady did ever actually die of a broken heart, perhaps popular imagination was in the last century more in tune with the facts than was the approach of conservative medicine with its mistrust of the thesis of self-induced disease. But even before the impact of Freud and his followers the view that the body ruled the mind, which had broadly prevailed since Plato's time, was moving back towards a point of dynamic equilibrium.

The history of medicine in the past century has been marked by a steady growth of the idea that many diseases are partly or wholly psychogenic. That far-sighted Scottish physician of the eighteenth century, William Cullen, made the sweeping claim that 'almost the whole of the diseases of the human body might be called nervous': as early as 1825 tuberculosis was associated with grief by both doctors and laymen: and a little later a French scientist attributed many disorders of the circulation and digestion to nervous tension. Asthma was recognized before the

First World War as belonging to this group, and has since been joined by other 'allergic' and skin diseases such as eczema. Nearly forty years ago Franz Alexander developed earlier work by relating peptic ulcers to mental conflict, and other forms of ulcer, benign tumours (eighty per cent of them on one reckoning) and malignant diseases were suspected of falling into this category. More recently migraine, coronary thrombosis, diabetes and possibly rheumatic and bronchial disorders and vasomotor rhinitis (nasal catarrh and blockage) have also been brought under the heading of 'stress diseases'.

The materialist who claims that *no* case of *any* of these can *ever* be induced by a mental state is now becoming rarer than the opposite extremist – for instance, the 'Christian Scientist' who claims that *all* cases of them are *always* caused by it. We do not need to agree with the attributing of one case of cancer in three to unhappiness (and Sir Heneage Ogilvie, the distinguished surgeon, has gone further and claimed that 'the happy man never gets cancer') to accept that very frequently anxiety lowers defences and increases vulnerability to disease at the body's point of least resistance. Carl Binger recently suggested that more people were sick because they were unhappy than vice versa, and Dr D. J. West has stated that 'psychological influence plays some part in almost all illnesses and a large part in many'.

In a still more surprising class are those instances in which, for example, one identical twin suffers the pain of the other's wounds, a husband shares his wife's labour pains or a medium suffers with his subject. One hesitates to mention such cases, since they invite considerations which would make this book unwieldy and leave it open to the charge of explaining *ignotum per ignotius*. But if true they would not be irrelevant to this story.

Disturbances of body state or function may hence be

explained in terms of mental mechanisms, usually unconscious. In the condition known as 'conversion hysteria' – which of course has nothing to do with religious conversion – emotional states are translated into physical terms: for instance, a man with a guilty secret is struck dumb as a defence against disclosing it or a woman with overwhelming troubles cannot keep her eyes open (that is, face life). A British communist at the time of Russia's crushing of the Hungarian bid for freedom lost his sight – he could not bear to face the facts – and during the last war I received into my military neurosis centre in North Africa two patients, recently in action, one of whom was functionally blind and the other deaf. Emotive phrases such as 'starved of affection' or 'itching for revenge' can be acted out by the body, so that a paralysis such as Pascal suffered may have been an expression of 'not knowing which way to turn'. Also accepted as psychological in origin are most of the cases in which over-pious Catholics have developed on their bodies temporary replicas of the stigmata of Christ's suffering.

There are four points which we should note here. One is that these examples of 'syndrome shift' are not necessarily against the patient's interest: after a broken love affair it may be better to develop asthma than to suffer despair, and the healer who removes symptoms without attacking the cause of a disease may be screwing down a valuable safety valve. However, recent studies of behaviour therapy (which is a therapeutic attack on symptoms rather than causes) indicate that this risk may be considerably less than was hitherto believed.

Secondly, we are now considering only physical and mental processes. Whether there is a separate class of spiritual maladies is another matter again, and one which – together with discussions of the existence of the soul or the psyche – we must leave to theologians. Even these latter, though – some of whom have welcomed the new medical knowledge as giving them a chance to explain away parts of the gospel which they find hard to accept – do not always seem clear on the place of the soul in therapy. Dr Weatherhead, for instance, appears to suggest that prayer, the panacea for all ills in orthodox doctrine (though one whose results have never been validated other than by the voice of faith) can be positively harmful in some disorders and that it may increase a sense of guilt which would be better dealt with by psychological methods.

In the third place, I am not suggesting that mentally-generated diseases of whatever type are in any sense trivial. Whether, as in hysterical conversion, psychological stress produces only symptoms without organic change or, as in psychosomatic conditions, it induces detectable alterations of physical state, they are often as far beyond the patient's control, and as distressing, as purely physical ones.

Finally, the fact that apparently physical diseases can be produced by non-physical causes is no *proof* that the reverse applies and that they can be relieved by non-physical methods. Reversible reactions are, however, the rule rather than the exception in science and we should hence be predisposed towards the possibility that (as Delboeuf wrote nearly a century ago) the conviction that a morbid condition did not exist might contribute to its disappearance. In fact, we do not even have to look as far as the experience of one young physician short of patients who increased his practice by inventing a wholly imaginary disease and curing it with great success by injections of distilled water, to argue that such is the case.

For, from classic times onwards, physicians have rarely hesitated to admit to themselves if not to their patients that a convincing 'bedside manner' speeds recovery, and to instill into their students the importance of a display of quiet confidence in any mode of treatment. The usefulness of the 'placebo' – whether it be a bottle of coloured water, a round-the-world cruise, a friendly word or, above all, the self-assurance of the therapist – has rarely been underrated. Fifty years ago the physician Sir William Osler, replying to the claims of the 'Christian Scientists', said that his professional experience had been that of an unconscious faith healer; and in recent literature general practitioners have estimated that as much as one third of the illness they deal with includes a psychological factor and is hence susceptible to the security, conscious or unconscious, promised by 'faith healing'.

In fact, for nearly a century physicians have been as increasingly unwilling to limit the curative power of suggestion as they have been increasingly willing to confess its causative potential. Almost the last words of Louis Pasteur, for instance, were to the effect that the microbe mattered less than the mental and physical ground in which it was let loose, while a little later a leading British surgeon said that his personality did more to heal than did his knife. From the other side of the fence, one faith healer who believes in the existence of paranormal powers considers that in four cases out of five the simple allaying of anxiety has played a part in his cures.

Little is known concerning the physical and psychological mechanisms by which the command that a sufferer should become well passes through that psychophysical complex which is man. Clues as to the former, however, are being assembled from an increasing knowledge of the close relationship between endocrinology, biochemistry and pharmacology. And meanwhile everyday experience is enough to inform us of the powerful and immediate, if transitory, links which exist between our emotions and our physiological responses; for phrases such as 'sweating with fear', 'butterflies in the stomach', 'fainting with emotion' and so forth are simply lay descriptions of short-lived changes in the blood pressure, pulse rate, state of the sweat glands or digestive and respiratory rhythms. (Some of these changes are, of course, measured by the so-called 'lie detector' which is in fact an emotion detector.) In themselves such physiological reactions to emotionally-toned experience do not explain the long-term processes of illness and recovery, but they are a daily rebuttal of any absolute dualism in our concepts of 'mind' and 'body'.

Certainly it is possible that, for one who has long been bed-ridden, the excitement of a journey to Lourdes or to a Cornish osteopath may release therapeutic agents into the body-mind complex. From a psychological standpoint, meanwhile, it has been suggested that surrender to *any* external power reduces sickness-creating strains. Perhaps more knowledge is needed before the physician who is unhappy without the type of evidence which can be examined through a microscope or in a test tube will be wholly satisfied about the validity of cures by suggestion. But for myself – and I am sure I speak for an increasing majority of my colleagues – I am convinced that such cures, ranging from the frequent and trivial to the rare and dramatic, do occur through normal, if barely understood, reactions between mind and body.

It may be relevant here to mention G. A. Kelly's argument that we ought not to think in terms of 'physiological events' as differing from 'psychological events' but rather of the same events as being physiologically or psychologically construed. This, of course, raises questions of semantics, and it may be that we are impeded in our understanding because history has tended towards the use of different 'languages' for the physical and the mental.

It would probably be accepted that the unconventional

healer receives more than the conventional physician's share of patients who are in an abnormal state of suggestibility. Reasonably enough, spiritual healers lay considerable stress on the fact that they deal with an above-average proportion of 'incurables' and 'cast-offs' – those on whom every orthodox, and sometimes a number of fringe, therapeutic techniques seem to have failed. But they are less ready to admit that sufferers in this state, apparently offered a last chance, may be in a position to draw on some reserve of recuperative power which was not called into operation by earlier orthodox treatment. For the latter is rarely dramatic: indeed, medical practice may too often err in the direction of forcing the patient into a position of passive acquiescence to, rather than active participation in, his own cure.

I am not suggesting that all or even the majority of healers rely on their patients' suggestibility: on the contrary, the overtly theatrical element appears to be on the decrease. Both table-turning Spiritualists and quasi-Christian hot-gospellers still prosper, but the norm either inside or outside the churches is rather the bedside visit or a consultation at a 'sanctuary'. However, even healers such as Mr Edwards (in many ways a quiet and level-headed man) often, and no doubt for the most well-intentioned of reasons, hold mass meetings.

We have seen that these are in essence as old as faith healing itself; but though the theme of mass emotionalism runs through history from before the crusades, the present post-Hitlerian generation is perhaps more aware than any other that a reasonable man cannot always be multiplied by ten thousand and remain reasonable. In particular, it is difficult to preserve a critical outlook when everyone present is claiming to have received immediate benefit. One wishes to conform: one puts on an act: one finds oneself in the situation known as 'role playing'. This latter state, which has come in for a good deal of attention from psychologists recently, is one in which a certain pattern of behaviour is worked out without any loss of the self-critical faculties, let alone of consciousness.

The condition formerly known as hysterical pregnancy, for instance, can be regarded as a woman's acting out of the desire for motherhood. Recent studies of rats too would seem to indicate that in their territorial battles these animals play out the role of 'the defeated' to the extent of dying without organic cause. But everyday experience alone is enough to suggest that much of our behaviour can be explained in terms of role playing. The conduct of people at a wedding, a funeral, a job interview, in court-ship or in battle is often so clearly influenced by their idea of what is appropriate in these contexts that we could come close to writing the script in advance. Over the past thirty years attempts have been made to explore the mech-anisms and extent of role playing, and it is increasingly argued that it is a function of social awareness and of what people expect of each other in inter-personal relationships.

For psychologists themselves, one of the most startling extensions of the role-playing thesis has been Rosenthal's contention that in their investigations both experimenter and subject tended to fall into 'role' relationships which affected the outcome of an experiment. In a long series of experiments, which were apparently models of design, Rosenthal showed that to a large extent the investigator was getting what he wanted. This is not to say that he was consciously 'cooking the books' but rather that his ex-pectations were somehow communicated to the subject. Thus experimenters (that is, experimenters in their own eyes but subjects from Rosenthal's point of view) who were told that their subjects were slow or fast learners turned in slow or fast learning results respectively, though the groups were in fact as closely equated as possible.

Similarly, early experiments in sensory deprivation which involved placing subjects into situations where there was virtually no auditory, visual or tactile stimulation aroused great interest because the subjects showed a kind of disorientation, sometimes accompanied by hallucinations. Later experiments, however, showed that similar effects could be achieved by putting subjects into an environment in which they were not sensorily deprived but in which the simple presence of a 'panic button' which they could push if the experimental situation became intolerable caused them to expect dramatic and novel personal experiences.

In itself role playing does not offer an adequate explanation of the kind of phenomenon we have been discussing; but it does suggest an avenue worth exploration. It can be argued that 'illness' is to some extent a role, in that patients and doctors have ideas (whether they are conscious of them or not) about appropriate behaviour in the context – and similarly that patient and faith healer have equally deep-rooted ideas about what they expect of themselves and what others expect of them. Furthermore such an attitude, once adopted, is hard to abandon. The healers themselves make some play of the fact that the reticent, agnostic Englishman is more likely to conceal the fact that he believes he has been cured by the supernatural than to boast of it; but conversely it can be argued that his desire to talk about spiritual 'operations' is stronger than such misgivings, and that though our language has no word for it most of us would enjoy the situation of being *miraculé*.

Suggestion, then, is a recognized psychological mechanism and many of the more thoughtful healers admit that it must play a part in their apparent successes. (One may again mention here the French investigator Maurice Colinon, who posed as a faith healer and had considerable

success with methods in which he himself had no credence.) The long-term value of suggestion is, however, very
disputable. If cancer could indeed be cured by psychological methods then obviously we would have a technique of
greater value than the most sophisticated surgery and the
patient would scarcely be concerned that his cure had not
derived from the surgeon, from God or from a healing
spirit. But the experience of medicine is rather that the
whole range of suggestive techniques is more successful
in relieving symptoms than in eliminating their origins.

This returns us to the theme of hypnotism, which we
left at some time after 1840 when mesmerism had passed
its peak. A few years later James Braid, a Manchester physician whose reputed adherence to phrenology prejudiced
his chances of acceptance by the orthodox, attempted to
strip the subject of both its mystical overtones and its
mechanistic undertones and gave it its present name.
Without pretending to *understand* hypnotism, he suggested that the fatiguing of the subject's eye muscles caused
by concentrating on a suitable object at an appropriate
distance might lead to a general relaxation of tensions and
so to an increased degree of acquiescence to commands.

Braid, indeed, revealed a clear appreciation of the poten-
tialities and limitations of hypnosis. The showmanlike
effects achieved by the Mesmer school were, he believed,
real enough and not due to collusion or deception; but
nor were they due to the superior will of the man in
charge. One could forget both mystery and magnets, since
all that was essential was a focus for the subject's attention; and even passes – it has been commented – now became *passés*.

Hypnotism could, Braid considered, prove a very important agent in the healing art, though he rejected the
idea of its being or ever becoming a universal remedy.
'By the impression which hypnotism induces on the

nervous system,' he wrote, 'we acquire a power of rapidly curing many functional diseases most intractable or altogether incurable by ordinary remedies.' But he stressed that hypnotism should not be used for its curiosity value, nor even for therapeutic purposes unless under medical supervision.

Unfortunately no final insight has been gained into the basic mechanism of hypnosis in the century and a quarter which has elapsed since Braid formed these eminently sane views and – despite orthodox scepticism – used hypnosis to induce and remove dramatic symptoms and perhaps to cure some patients of rheumatism and migraine. Three Frenchmen, in the second half of the last century, struggled with the problem without greatly illuminating it, partly on account of their personal loyalties and antipathies; these were A. A. Liébeault, Hippolite Bernheim (who stressed that hypnotism was only a deep form of suggestibility) and J. M. Charcot. Charcot, who lived from 1825 to 1893, became interested towards the end of his life in faith healing; and it is of some interest in the history of abnormal psychology that he used magnetic machines even while acting as tutor to the young Sigmund Freud.

In general medical practice, however, hypnosis was found useful for inducing analgesia and anaesthesia. After the middle of the last century it was gradually superseded by chemicals, which could not only be more accurately administered and controlled but which appeared more acceptable and less bizarre in the eyes of orthodox practitioners. But for the past hundred years it has retained a place in the armoury of psychological and physical medicine, varying in popularity from time to time but generally accepted despite such rearguard actions from the ultra-conservative as delayed its recognition by the British Medical Association until 1955.

Perhaps there is a more general consensus within the medical profession, and a more accurate appreciation by the public, of the psychological than the therapeutic manifestations of hypnotism. It is accepted, for instance, that under deep hypnosis (which has been called 'a third estate of the mind intermediate between wakefulness and sleep') memories normally beyond the range of consciousness may be recalled and the senses easily deceived. That black could appear as white to the hypnotized subject was known in classical times, and it is as easy to persuade such a subject that salt tastes sweet and that a light object is intolerably heavy. Curiously enough, the moral conscience appears generally to survive the loss of other self-critical faculties: the hypnotized subject will readily believe that a glass of water contains sulphuric acid but will reject the hypnotist's suggestion that he should throw it in another's face. Indeed, such a suggestion would probably awaken him.

Some, but not all, subjects, were they to spill such 'sulphuric' water on their hands, might develop burn reactions similar to those produced by real sulphuric acid. Puzzling as these phenomena are, there is no doubt at all that on this level mind and body interact in spectacular ways which cannot readily be duplicated except in a hypnotic trance. Tell a suggestible subject that the ruler which you hand him is a red hot poker, for instance, and he may develop a superficial reddening resembling a burn, though much less severe than any hot poker would actually produce, and painless (unless specific post-hypnotic suggestion was added) when normal consciousness was regained.

There is little doubt that such performances can be conducted in reverse, so that subjects can survive contact with hot objects without showing the normal reactions of pain or burning. This fact doubtless underlines many of the fakir's demonstrations. Other physical powers can also be increased to a remarkable degree under hypnosis: for instance, the stage hypnotist's trick of supporting a man with his neck and ankles on chair backs and then standing on his chest involves no deception of the audience.

In the light of this there seems no *prima facie* reason to reject claims that other bodily processes, normally beyond the control of the mind, can also be affected by hypnotic suggestion. It is possible, for instance, for the blood pressure to be influenced under hypnosis and the pulse rate too can be significantly altered: yogis have long regarded this as a novice's exercise. It also seems acceptable that in a highly suggestible state a subject can emulate the mystic's device of 'sweating blood' through the pores of the skin. There is good but not conclusive evidence that digestive processes, and even the rate of manufacture of blood corpuscles, can be influenced by hypnotic suggestion. Hypnosis has also been employed to reduce congestion in the mucous membrane of the nose, and the associated colour change from red to pink has been photographed.

Despite this wide range of effects, many physicians are wary of introducing hypnosis into their regular practice: they argue that the effects are too shallow, too variable and too little understood for it to be employed where there is a recognized alternative. In the avoidance of pain it has proved useful in the preparation for dental operations, for changing the dressings of severely burned patients and in childbirth. But its actual therapeutic effects have proved generally disappointing, though some workers (notably Dr Griffith Edwards) have had considerable success with asthma and in 1952 Dr A. Mason reported the unique cure by hypnosis of a skin disease previously thought to be intractable.

Facsimiles of burns and other minor lesions, for instance, may be readily induced by suggestion, but the healing of true burns is only accelerated to a limited degree by such treatment. The text books and medical journals abound with cases of more serious illness of almost every type in which hypnotic treatment appears to have played a part in the cure, and many psychiatrists have reported series of patients whose recovery from functional disorders has been facilitated by hypnosis. But it is certainly no cure-all.

Many, indeed, would regard as an overstatement even Dr Weatherhead's claim that 'if the mind really accepts and believes ... that disease is being overcome, that health is returning and that [these] ideas are reasonable then, in ways that seem miraculous ... the mind gets its ideas carried out in the body and health is restored'. But there is no doubt that – if in a somewhat arbitrary fashion – hypnotism can produce startling short-term effects with a sprinkling of more enduring ones, and these must account for a proportion of the faith healer's apparent successes.

It is not suggested that the healer frequently and consciously employs hypnotic techniques: on the contrary, they are probably commoner in orthodox than in unorthodox practice. But in any activity which takes place in an emotionally-charged atmosphere (and particularly when mass meetings are involved) cases of self-induced hypnosis may well occur. And when they do they can lead to superficially impressive results.

The use of the phrase 'self-induced' hypnosis leads on to an allied type of phenomenon. It is, of course, possible for a subject to reach a highly suggestible state simply by concentrating on a platform speaker: even a point of light will serve. And similarly the suggestion need not come from outside the subject: it may be one consciously or unconsciously held in his own mind.

Recovery through auto-suggestion need not even depend on a sub-hypnotic state: it may occur at moments of intense shock. It has been noted throughout medical history that 'the shock of a violent reaction takes the nerve centres by storm' so that, for instance, a man bedridden with paralysis for years may, at an alarm of 'Fire!', not merely run for his life but carry heavy possessions with him – and possibly remain cured thereafter. Nearly a thousand years ago the great Avicenna cured the spinal curvature of a modest Moslem girl by saying that he could do nothing for her until she removed her skirt: Sir Humphry Davy noted that a clinical thermometer was a lifesaver to those who ignorantly mistook it for such: a Frenchman dying of tuberculosis rose from his bed to fight in the defence of his city and not only survived but was permanently cured: an asthmatic who believed he would stifle without the bedroom window open awoke in the night to find it closed, got up to open it, took great gulps of air, returned to bed and slept soundly until in the morning he found that he had opened the face of a grandfather clock and not the window: these are some of the classic-anecdotal cases of mind-body interaction. An instance involving a healthy man was witnessed when a U.S.N. lieutenant during a submarine attack carried up on deck a safe containing secret papers which normally took four men to lift. 'That was no miracle,' commented an onlooker, 'that was adrenalin and hysteria.'

The technique of cure by deliberate self-persuasion is associated with the name of Coué, a self-taught apothecary of Nancy who was born in 1857 but did not receive great public attention until the present century. Coué believed that auto-suggestion could produce results comparable with those of the faith healers, and attributed the powers of the latter entirely to hetero-suggestion. His methods, relying on the iteration of such phrases – reminiscent of the 'positive thinking' of the American school – as 'Every day in every way I am getting better and better', certainly involved a measure of self-deception which led to their eventual abandonment. (It is also probable that in many cases they also involved a measure of self-hypnosis, though Coué denied this.) But they enjoyed a considerable measure of popularity and success around 1910, when Coué was personally instructing up to one hundred patients daily and claiming cures not only of psychological states but of appendicitis and gout: and they were revived in the inter-war period and are not yet forgotten by those who believe that 'all cures are self-cures'.

At least one more point should be made concerning suggestibility in general, which is that its value as a therapeutic agent seems to depend as much on the healer's faith in his methods as on that of the patient. (This principle, of course, underlies the 'double-blind' method of randomization which is now recognized as necessary in the evaluation of new drugs.) There is evidence, for instance, that many cures of warts work only if the physician himself is convinced of their efficacy – a fact of orthodox medicine which it is interesting to compare with the healer's belief that his powers will wane if he puts a profitable price on his services.

After such considerations, the number of miscellaneous alternative explanations which are adduced by sceptics to cast doubt on the validity of particular 'miracle cures' fall into rather simpler categories. First, perhaps, comes the possibility of what is known to physicians as spontaneous remission – a more or less permanent arresting or reversing of the course of a disease which, though frequently met with as in leukaemia, is inexplicable in the current state of knowledge. Although numerous medical men consider that the term 'incurable' is in any case overemployed, it does not preclude the possibility that a disease may remit spontaneously. As with every aspect of this subject, one would welcome more reliable information; but for cancer – a disease often 'incurable' in the sense of being fatal by the time it is diagnosed – there is evidence that in between one in 10,000 and one in 100,000 cases pain ceases, damage to tissues is halted and even reversed, and the patient enjoys many more years of useful life.

Dr Michael Balint, who considers such cases to be comparable to the results obtained at Lourdes, describes the problem posed by such remissions as 'frightening and uncanny'. 'We doctors,' he continues, 'have no idea whether the recovery was due to us or to some power beyond our control,' and he rightly calls for more statistics on spontaneous remission. What is certain, however, is that *some* such incidents must coincide with visits to faith healers of various schools. Indeed, it has been suggested by the healers that such remissions are never truly spontaneous but are brought on, unknown to the patient, by absent prayer. According to Mr Edwards, this may even implant a 'hunch' in the surgeon's mind or direct his hands.

Furthermore, we must remember that – as Mesmer knew – in a number of diseases such as multiple sclerosis the patient's symptoms and general physical state follow an oscillating, if generally descending, curve whose periodicity may be a matter of years. Each plunge into sickness is followed by an apparent rise towards health – and a number of these respites will coincide with a visit to an unorthodox healer who will claim and receive the credit for them. The subsequent reversions to a state worse than before tend to escape attention but are part of the natural history of disease.

This, in turn, raises the question of the permanency of the cures attributed to unorthodox as opposed to orthodox treatment. Unfortunately, we are here once more brought up against a vagueness of terminology. Orthodox medicine does not care for the term 'cure', recognizing that every disease can only be certainly terminated by a patient's death – perhaps from very different causes. The patient himself, though, is more sympathetic to the lay healer's view that, if he feels better for a few months, then he *is* better.

Next we should note that, as Harry Edwards has recognized, the condition of most of the healer's patients is known to him – and thence, perhaps, to the press – by little more than hearsay. It is certainly not unusual for sufferers to mistake or overdramatize their condition, possibly after having overheard, in a not-unreasonable state of acute nervousness and suggestibility, a hospital discussion referring to a quite different patient. Certainly the proportion of 'case histories' on the files of healers containing the words 'my doctor could do no more for me' seems suspiciously large in an age when new methods of treatment are always being attempted and when hope is not as easily abandoned as in the days when Belloc wrote of medical specialists, 'They answered as they took their fees, There is no cure for this disease.'

Much of the labour of conventional physicians is devoted to the keeping of records such as case histories: this is essential in the interests of both the patient and medical knowledge as a whole. The faith healer, on the other hand, rarely has the time, inclination, staff, resources or even temperament for such documentation, with the result that any dialogue between the two tends to proceed at cross purposes. It is reasonable for the physician to object that a 'healing by faith' happened too far in the past for the relevant records to be available, just as it is to object that another occurred too recently to be confirmed as complete. Perhaps it is no less reasonable for the faith healer to ask within what time limits the medical confirmation of a cure *is* possible; but certainly the time factor is important in this context.

Rather more controversial is the readiness of orthodox

physicians to claim, in refutation of a purported paranormal cure, that their records have been lost or X-ray prints misattributed. Such incidents are not likely to inspire confidence. But, inevitably if rarely, they *do* occur; and the more puzzling a condition is, the more likely are the case notes to be studied by many workers in different hospitals and departments. Similarly, there *are* cases of mistaken diagnosis: many of the healers' successes are, in essence, no more than the refutation of the predictions of an under-experienced and overworked practitioner. It is certainly unfortunate that the entire resources of modern medical science cannot be brought to bear on every case of sickness; but in the nature of things they are not.

Again, it is often far from clear whether, in a purported case of paranormal healing, ordinary medical treatment had in fact been abandoned: even when it *is* clear, the possibility remains that earlier conventional methods had an unusually delayed effect. In yet other cases, it is obvious that the patient had been too sick to report on his own condition with any reliability. These and other possibilities (such as the possible involvement of telepathic or other extrasensory powers), as well as the familiar ones of suggestion, spontaneous remission, mistaken diagnoses and the rest, must all be taken into account when we are evaluating the successes of the faith healers.

But, even so, the general objections discussed above no more tell the full story than do the uncritical reports of the Spiritualist press. We may not yet be prepared to agree with Dr Thouless that 'there *is* a capacity for paranormal healing' or with Brian Inglis that 'the innumerable healing episodes on record are more easily explained by assuming the existence of a healing force than by all the "scientific" rationalizations'. But we must recognize that the mass of evidence presented earlier in this book will not be disposed of by the series of stories about lost X-ray plates which have been too common in the approach of orthodox medicine to unorthodox cures – and that it is a mass which calls for respect if not outright credence.

What is needed if we are to arrive at the truth, I believe, is not more affirmation of creeds, more sensationalized 'human stories', more vague but massive committees with obscure terms of reference, more blasts of unyielding scepticism, more claims such as 'thirty per cent of my patients get better', more attempts at the mechanical measurement of healing forces or even more investigations (such as Professor Servadio would seem to favour) of the healer's personality. The demand is rather for a painstaking examination of actual cases to see if any cures remain which cannot reasonably be explained on the basis of the principles considered in this chapter.

# PART TWO

## CHAPTER SIX

## Investigation

COMPARING herself to St Mark, Miss Sibyl Wilbur – the official biographer of Mary Baker Eddy – claimed that she aimed to set out the facts of divine healing in a 'direct and unvarnished way': it was not for her, she said, 'to explain or expound'. Having stated this, she went on to write the type of propagandist work typical of a good deal of the literature of faith healing.

I would like to think that this book does not betray so biased an approach, but so far it has certainly been lacking in the type of data which would enable an unprejudiced person to reach a valid conclusion as to the reality of faith cures. What, in fact, can the literature of over two thousand years offer us in the form of 'scientific' evidence on the subject?

We would not expect to find such evidence dating from much more than two centuries back, though it is interesting to note that at his coronation Louis XIV of France touched 2,400 invalids and that, after an 'investigation of sorts' (in the words of Carl Scherzer), it was concluded that only five sufferers benefited. I have also mentioned one or two attempts made somewhat later – attempts perhaps legalistic rather than strictly scientific in their approach – to subject faith healers of various persuasions to the ordinary disciplines of evidence: there were, for instance, the examinations of Mesmer and of von Hohenlohe after him. These seem in general to have cast doubts on the healers' philosophies if only through their self-contradictions, without disposing of – or even tentatively confirming – the possible reality of the cures themselves.

Little else in the way of examination seems to have been undertaken until, early in the present century, a group of two Anglican priests and one physician of the Emmanuel movement in the USA (a movement, mentioned earlier, which was set up by the Episcopalian church after it had been inspired to a renewed interest in healing by the work of the 'Christian Scientists') established a home outside Boston for the treatment of tuberculous slum-dwellers by rest, fresh air and prayer. This was so successful, at least in removing such symptoms as haemorrhage and cough, that the city health authorities copied it – omitting, however, the element of prayer. It appears that without this last component the regime was, in the state of medical knowledge at that time, of so little use that the secular approach was abandoned, while the religious one continued to show good results.

There are, of course, several possible explanations for this difference. But after sixty years this remains one of the very few comparisons ever attempted between two groups of sufferers, with one group receiving all the attention given to the other *plus* a 'paranormal' element. In this case, the latter was the faith on the part of both healer and healed in the effectiveness of divine intervention.

Since ethical considerations may prevent the denial to a patient of any aid to health with some claims to efficacy and no undesirable effects, the statistical evaluation of the usefulness of paranormal healing – as of many drugs – must in part be based on such almost-accidental concatenations of experience. No clinical researcher, for instance, could forbid private prayers being offered up for his patients. Controlled tests in the strictest sense can perhaps never be carried out on human subjects (although one investigator has tried to heal mice in an experimental situation), and an attempt to bring a scientific approach to the purported phenomena of paranormal healing is not helped by the fact that not only medical ethics but religious susceptibilities are involved.

'God does not submit to test-tube experiments' has been the claim of many healers in the Catholic tradition; and Dr Day, a thoughtful American Methodist, has expressed the view that 'the presence of an investigator breathing down one's neck ... would destroy that un-self-consciousness so essential in true spiritual healing'. Individual healers, such as the Reverend Cameron Peddie whose blood pressure measurements have been referred to earlier and d'Angelo who appeared in carefully-supervised tests to have produced a 'psychic wind' measured by an anemometer, have submitted to various forms of rather inconclusive experiments. But Frederick Knowles, a Canadian who practised faith healing before he qualified as a physician, seems to have shown that even such paranormal gifts as he believed he possessed vanished under laboratory conditions; and in general all who claim psychic powers feel inhibited by experimental conditions so that their phenomena are rarely experienced or produced.

Yet despite such difficulties two types of inquiry could be attempted to assess the claims of the paranormal healers. One is the statistical type crudely adumbrated in the 'Emmanuel experiment' and since recommended by Professor Alstead and others: we should look for groups of sufferers as similar as possible except that one was being subjected to some form of paranormal treatment and the other not, and compare the results. The other method would be closer to the *experimentum crucis* beloved of traditional science and described by Paracelsus as 'a spear to thrust, a club to batter'. Statistical in its own way, it would involve the examination of the alleged 'miracle cures' of the healers in order to determine whether more would stand up to close examination than could be reasonably dismissed on the grounds discussed in the last chapter.

The statistical type of examination, even if the difficulties of finding suitable subjects were overcome, could obviously only be administered by a team of experts. It would, I believe, be a most valuable exercise if not a conclusive one, for as Dr Thouless has written concerning Harry Edwards, '6,000 weak testimonies do not necessarily add up to a convincing whole'. (Concerning both types of test and referring to the same healer, Dr Thouless has said that 'if either gave positive results, it would not be certain that all doctors would believe in the reality of Mr Edwards' healing. It would then be possible, however, to claim that the evidence was such that they ought to believe in it'. But I know of only one recent attempt along such lines, and even that is open to criticism in some respects.

It was carried out in Freiburg, Germany, under the direction of Dr Inge Strauch; Dr Hans Rehder and Professor Hans Bender also collaborated. For six months in 1955, 650 volunteer patients – with a predominance of elderly women – visited the Institute of Psychology and Psycho-hygiene and were also treated by a Dr Kurt Trampler who believed in healing through the rapport of spiritual energy between himself and his subjects. The illnesses dealt with included disorders of the heart and circulation, bone diseases, and rheumatic, neurological and intestinal ailments: nearly three quarters of the total were classed as 'organic' and all had failed to show any notable improvement as a result of orthodox treatment – which, nevertheless, was continued in about two thirds of the cases.

A breakdown of the results showed that 'subjective' improvement was reported in sixty-one per cent of the cases which passed through the healer's hands, but that twenty-two per cent improved only temporarily and ten per cent actually deteriorated. Most of the nine per cent of 'objective' improvements were in cases of gastro-intestinal illness – and here, it seemed, conventional treatment was equally effective. In general, a positive correlation was found between the effectiveness of the healer's treatment and the degree of the sufferer's credence in it: the typical patient who reacted positively, for instance, tended to be a rather unsophisticated country-dweller, slow-thinking but with an optimistic temperament, placid and uncritical, cherishing religious superstitions and more likely to believe in magical 'rays' than in the efficacy of suggestion. In one interesting subsidiary experiment a small group was told that absent healing would be given at a certain time when in fact it was not: most of this group reported that they *felt* better though their physical state was not improved.

Turning to the second and more critical type of inquiry, this would of course have its own limitations. It might not – and to the committed believer it certainly *would* not – confirm a negative verdict on the reality of paranormal healing; but it might well confirm a positive one. If, out of a hundred examples of the faith healer's art, we found not just a single apparently remarkable cure which *might* still be explained on orthodox grounds but a small group of them, then for the first time there would be evidence that such phenomena were to be taken very seriously. The same technique might later be used to distinguish between, say, the efficacy of Christian and of Spiritualist methods.

This type of investigation does appear a possible undertaking for a single individual or small group. However, apart from an inquiry into two 'healing missions' made by the Church of England in the 1920s (after which Canon L. W. Grensted commented that 'letters sent to every doctor and to every clergyman in the districts concerned failed to produce any information as to the real nature of definitely organic cases [though] there was plenty of evidence of the cure of "functional" disorders'), I have found only one account of such an inquiry. This was conducted by the Rev. Bertram Woods, who investigated some cases submitted to the Society for Psychical Research.

Mr Woods met profound difficulties in following up even the limited number of instances which were brought to his notice, difficulties of a kind with which any worker in this field becomes familiar: typical of these were the reluctance of patients to tell their physicians that they had been receiving unorthodox treatment (and of some sympathetic physicians to declare their sympathy publicly), the apparent refusal of faith healers to supply concrete facts to those willing to take up the challenges which they themselves issued, and vague terminology of the type which led the Earl of Sandwich – an eccentric faith healer who practised at the end of the last century – to call any patient 'cured' who did not actually die. In the event, Mr Woods elicited only six claims of dramatic cures – all from one psychic healer – and, though himself a believer in divine therapy, found only one case worthy of serious interest.

This work, however, had not even begun when at the beginning of 1951 Mrs K. M. Goldney, the then honorary secretary of the Society for Psychical Research, suggested that, as a clinical psychiatrist, I might be interested in attending a demonstration of faith healing. Mr Harry Edwards was at that time holding mass meetings in various parts of Britain at the rate of about one a fortnight, and one had been arranged at the Kingsway Hall, Holborn, on 10 March 1951. Later, Dr Thouless (who is, of course, a non-medical investigator) was to write of 'Britain's Number One "Healer"' that 'without much more detailed research [it would be] impossible to give proof convincing to a sceptic that any paranormal process is at work. I think that most probably it is,' continued Dr Thouless, 'but there is no reason why the sceptical doctor should accept my opinion.' I was, apparently, to be cast for the role of that sceptical doctor.

In summary, I found Mr Edwards' approach pleasantly free of mystification or deliberate attempts to trade on suggestibility. On the other hand – as mentioned in the previous chapter – there is inevitably an immense pressure to conform when one is a member of a mass audience of which most are in rapport with each other and with the demonstrator. Indeed, I confirmed this from personal experience when Mr Edwards asked me to agree that a young man whom he was about to treat was suffering from scoliosis, or curvature of the spine.

Although I expected this request, I was surprised that there was no opportunity for even a cursory examination. I was simply asked to verify that the youth was suffering from spasticity of the spinal muscles; and I was on the point of agreeing when I realized that to have done so would have been purely a response to expectation. I had made no proper examination of the sufferer and, from what little I could feel through his clothing, 'spasticity' was not a word which could be correctly applied. After that one instance, I was not invited to collaborate further in the demonstration.

Also at this meeting occurred the incident, mentioned earlier, of the woman who left the platform walking freely but whom I met on the pavement outside relying on her sticks again. But the fact remains that many dozens of sufferers from arthritis and similar diseases – a high proportion of whom stated that their complaints had long resisted orthodox treatment – *did* appear to have their disability at least temporarily ameliorated as a result of Mr Edwards' instructions and painless ministrations. (This fact, together with the subsequent relapses, has also been noted by Dr Thouless.) Certainly I became more interested in the healer's claims on the strength of my observations that day.

Later I attended other meetings of Mr Edwards', including one in September 1951 at the Royal Festival Hall, London, at which both the dramatic potential and Mr Edwards' degree of 'editing' of his patients' testimony seemed notably higher. For instance, Mr Edwards said to one sufferer, 'You couldn't lift that arm before, could you?' and she replied, 'Well, perhaps not as much.' The healer then turned to the audience with the words, 'She hasn't been able to move her arm for years.' Mr Edwards, when I commented on this after the meeting, explained, 'You must remember that this was a demonstration.' A journalist not unsympathetic to Spiritualism wrote later that 'as cure followed cure ... it was possible to sense the emotion generated in the audience'.

I also visited Mr Edwards' sanctuary at Shere, Surrey, where I was able to study his approach in more detail than at the mass meetings. There I formed at least one new impression – that whereas he generally rounded off his treatment of primarily organic diseases with the *hope* that the patient would improve, he was far more positive and confident when treating those patients of limited physical function with whom anyone familiar with the techniques of persuasion and suggestion would *expect* to induce temporary improvements. With these latter his parting words were more typically 'You will be better' or 'You are better now.'

After the Festival Hall meeting I had approached Mr Edwards, explaining that I was interested in discovering the truth concerning the efficacy of spiritual healing. I then solicited his help in submitting to me details of those cures which he considered impressive enough to convince any doubter. This was the beginning of a correspondence which has now spread over more than eighteen years. Since I have been working from an agnostic standpoint and Mr Edwards from that of a committed Spiritualist, the dialogue has at times been in danger of becoming sterile. But it has been kept alive by Mr Edwards' desire to convince me that he is right and by my own desire to reach a conclusion one way or the other; and I should stress that I have never found Mr Edwards deliberately evasive or mystery-making.

Here I should once more underline that what I was looking for was not assistance in a statistical task of a magnitude which would demand computer analysis but rather a handful of 'cures' which would satisfy standards similar to those laid down by the authorities of Rome and Lourdes – though, of course, without any theological complications. To recapitulate on these conditions, it is interesting to cite the criteria suggested by an American physician, Russell G. MacRobert, at about this time. He suggested that a paranormal cure could not be accepted as valid without sound diagnosis, the failure of the best orthodox medical and psychiatric treatment, the application of a psychic method and a subsequent recovery to the satisfaction of experts.

To draw an analogy from another realm of parapsychological research, I was less concerned with Dr Rhine's successful card-telling – which corresponds medically to a thousand instances of slight improvement – than with Swedenborg's single spectacular clairvoyance of the Stockholm fire. To demand miracles may sound a very tall order, especially considering the fact that as laymen the faith healers have not the access to medical histories available to the physicians of the *Bureau des Constatations*. Indeed, I could myself only have such access by courtesy of the patient and physician; and while cases of refusal have in the event proved rare, those where one party or another has not replied to letters or has been lost track of have amounted to as much as fifty per cent.

On the other hand, though, the word 'miracle' is frequently bandied about in the Spiritualist press (and remarkably frequently put into the mouths of doctors and surgeons), and Mr Edwards' own evaluation is that he is incomparably more successful than the whole apparatus of Lourdes. In the early 1950s, too, he was claiming that in the previous five years he had read a million letters. Assuming that each patient sent an average of three letters, and working on Mr Edwards' claim of a rate of complete success of about one patient in every three, there should have been living in Britain in 1952 something like 100,000 men, women and children who had received striking benefit at this healer's hands alone. If from these a mere ten cases emerged which satisfied the Lourdes standards – and which, preferably, were based on measurable data – then the case for faith healing would have been substantially proved. And even one case – just one out of 100,000 – would have given every thoughtful practitioner cause to ponder deeply.

Furthermore my appeal was not to Mr Edwards alone, though since he was (and remains) the leading faith healer of our age a selection from his 'case book' should surely provide a better-than-average proportion of success. For instance, I had hopeful expectations of Christopher Woodard, who in addition to being a faith healer was also a qualified medical man and a member of a disciplined church.

Accordingly I wrote to Dr Woodard asking for records of 'one case in which there has been specific improvement of a measurable organic condition after [faith] healing'. He wrote back to say that he would do what he could to help and would write again 'within a day or two'. Nine months later I wrote to remind him that a day or two had passed, and he replied most charmingly and invited me to lunch.

I naturally accepted, at the same time asking him to bring one case history with him. We had a very enjoyable lunch – but without any case histories. Dr Woodard explained that he was then writing another book and did not want to steal his own thunder, but that having met me and discovered how I was working he felt able to trust me; a couple of case-sheets, he promised, would reach me by the next post.

That was well over seventeen years ago. I have not yet received them.

Notices asking for information about successful cures were also published in the *Lancet* and the *British Medical Journal* under cross-heads drawing attention to the subject, and these must have been read by almost every English-speaking medical practitioner with an interest in the subject. I also followed up every report of a 'miracle' cure which came to my notice through the national and provincial press, and wrote to journalists such as Mr Beverley Nichols known to be interested in the subject. The plan underlying my investigation was to send a simple questionnaire to the subjects of these claims, inviting them to obtain the co-operation of their doctors. I hoped that in this way I might gather such details of their diseases as duration, the names of any hospitals attended, and the dates during which treatment had been given.

In the meantime, the word had been passed round and I began to get letters from all over the world from people telling me that they had been cured, that they knew of others who had been cured, or that they were themselves healers. The last group sent batches of letters from grateful patients or wrote their own accounts of patients they believed they had healed. I followed up every case and answered every letter personally, enclosing my question-naire. A fair proportion of the replies were clearly absurd, but others added usefully to my files of material.

I hence felt that I was exploring most of the avenues available to any single investigator working part-time. But meanwhile in the United States Mrs Eileen J. Garrett – a lady of commanding appearance and personality, a medium and a convinced believer in the reality of psychic phenomena – had wisely decided to devote her consider-able energies and resources, not to the forming of yet an-other Spiritualist sect, but to the sponsoring of genuinely disinterested inquiry into paranormal matters by highly qualified investigators. Shortly before, in fact, Mrs Garrett had set up the Parapsychology Foundation Inc. of New York, a body which – like the SPR – was interested in the whole spectrum of paranormal powers and manifesta-tions.

It was under the auspices of this lady and this founda-tion that there took place, at Utrecht in Holland and from 30 July to 5 August 1953, what appears to have been the first international gathering for over twenty years of those interested in the facets of human capacity and experience which seem to exist outside the range of the normal con-cepts of physical and medical science. Certainly this con-ference assembled together a remarkable constellation of talent, for the more than eighty delegates from fourteen countries who were selected for invitation and who in fact attended (Great Britain sending nearly a quarter of them), included virtually every scientist or layman of first-rank reputation in the field.

I was myself invited by reason of my known interest in paranormal healing, and my contribution was to pre-sent an interim report on the state of my inquiry up to that date. Inconclusive and perhaps negative as my find-ings were, they attracted considerable interest. And it was partly as a result of them that two Dutch representatives, Drs Kat and Kappers, suggested that the Parapsychology Foundation should set up an international verification centre for paranormal healings.

I considered this a most valuable proposal, and was happy to be asked – together with Dr Kat and the eminent psychiatrist Professor Urban of Innsbruck, Austria – to work with Mrs Garrett on exploring the possibilities. What we all had in mind, of course, was a body comparable to the Lourdes *Bureau des Constatations* – but without doctrinal preconceptions – which could bring the full battery of modern medical knowledge to bear on claims of cures achieved by paranormal means anywhere in the world. Such a body would be costly to maintain, and perhaps for that reason alone the project has been shelved and its realization seems even remoter today than it did at the time. But money has been found without great difficulty for much less potentially rewarding medical researches.

Another and firmer plan, however, also emerged from the Utrecht conference. This was that a further meeting should be held in the near future which should be devoted to the study of paranormal healing. Its members – known as the International Study Group on Unorthodox Healings – met from the 27 to the 30 April 1954 in the pleasant surroundings of St Paul de Vence near Nice.

I was surprised to find that, although the conference was ostensibly gathered for the study of faith healing in all its forms, the only member present whom I knew to have studied the healers' claims was the journalist Maurice Colinon who had (as mentioned previously) made some attempts to explore the field. Dr Leuret, the president of the *Bureau des Constatations* at Lourdes, was a member of the conference; but he had dealt only with the records of Lourdes and never with individual healers.

I was, therefore, in a position similar to that at the

Utrecht conference, in that I had done very little more and there was virtually nobody else who had done anything at all with whom I could compare notes. Furthermore, the agenda indicated that the intention of the conference was to study the various mechanisms by which paranormal cures were thought to have been achieved. The sponsors were intending to discuss the reasons why things happened when it had not yet been proved that they did.

I would disagree, for instance, even with Dr Eric Dingwall, who wrote: 'Today we seem almost in the same position as the sufferers in the temple of Aesculapius. Cures are effected: patients are relieved of their symptoms: apparently paranormal effects are produced – but how?' I felt we should explore the *whether* before worrying about the *how* and *why*, and that the whole situation was rather like that obtaining when eighteenth-century English savants debated by what magnetic devices Mahommet's coffin could be held suspended in mid-air until a traveller returned from Mecca with the news that it was not suspended at all.

So – as I mentioned at the start of this book – when the meeting opened with the pronouncement that its purpose was to discover what extrasensory factors were involved in paranormal healing, I interrupted to say that I considered that the cart was being put before the horse. Even the 1784 committee which investigated Mesmer, it is interesting to note, corrected its terms of reference when its members realized that it was useless to inquire whether the 'mesmeric force' could be used therapeutically before they were satisfied – as in the event they were *not* – that such a force existed. And the outcome was that, though I remained on cordial terms with many members of this group and had interesting discussions with them on various aspects of parapsychology, very little progress was made on the subject of healing.

Back in London again in the summer of 1954, I found a new call on my attention in that the Archbishops' Commission on Healing and the BMA were asking for the views of physicians on paranormal healing. Shortly afterwards (as has also been mentioned earlier) I gave to these bodies evidence which consisted in essence of an amplification of the material which I had presented in St Paul de Vence. Some of the case-studies reported in the next few pages in fact formed part of their *corpus*, and I was somewhat gratified when my evidence was described by the chairman of the parent commission as 'the first ray of light we have had' and by the chairman of the BMA sub-committee as 'a breath of fresh air'.

All the time, though, I continued the process – a painstaking, sometimes tedious, sometimes frustrating but always, I believed, worth-while process – of obtaining from healers the names and addresses of their more spectacular alleged successes and of attempting to follow up these claims (together with some more made in the press) by contacting the patients and physicians involved. I continually found new difficulties – for instance, for a cure to be accepted as miraculous it was obviously necessary that the sufferer had been receiving no orthodox treatment at the same time, which probably meant that there had been no examination by a physician close enough to the cure for a 'before and after' professional comparison to be drawn. But after more than two years I found that I had examined the documentation of just under one hundred cases, and the time seemed ripe for a review of the material. My paper on 'Paranormal Healing' appeared in the *British Medical Journal* in December 1954 and a somewhat amplified version, based on a lecture to the SPR, was published in the journal of that society in September 1955.

From the latter publication I think it is worth while quoting at some length (and almost verbatim) not only a summary of my findings but also twelve 'case histories' of various types of apparent cure, the latter being selected – now, as at the date of their first publication – for their variety and illustrative value. In essence, then, I analysed 95 instances of purported faith cures and found that (and here I quote):

(1) In 58 cases it was not possible to obtain medical or other records so that the claims remained unconfirmed:

(2) In 22 cases, records were so much at variance with the claims that it was considered useless to continue the investigation further:

(3) In 2 cases the evidence in the medical records suggested that the healer may have contributed to amelioration of an organic condition:

(4) In 1 case demonstrable organic disability was relieved or cured after intervention by the healer:

(5) 3 cases improved but relapsed:

(6) 4 cases showed a satisfactory degree of improvement in function although re-examination and comparison of medical records revealed no change in the organic state:

(7) In 4 cases there was improvement when healing was received concurrently with orthodox medical treatment:

(8) One case examined before and after treatment by the healer gained no benefit and continued to deteriorate.

Typical case histories follow.

(A) A child, V. T. (Group 1) was claimed to have responded miraculously to a healer and the name of the hospital where she had been treated unsuccessfully was obtained through the newspaper concerned. The parents were 'adamant in their refusal' to permit the records to be made available.

(B) Mr M. L. (Group 2), reported in the press as having been cured by Mr Edwards, wrote: 'I cannot claim to have derived any benefit as a result of that one visit, as that was more than two years ago and it is only in the past few weeks that I have felt any improvement: whether this is due to treatment I have received at the hospital clinic I cannot say.'

(C) Mrs M. H. (Group 2) was the subject of an article in a

well-known pictorial magazine: the patient sent in her own history. After several X-ray and anaesthetic examinations the hospital could do nothing more for her: she was discharged, she said 'presumably as incurable', in 1936. She had been obliged to continue wearing her surgical belt for thirteen more years and could not get out of bed without it, but in 1949 she went to a healer at whose hands she was 'cured'.

When I examined the hospital records, they revealed that Mrs M. H. had had an appendicectomy in 1934 and a curettage for cervical erosion. In 1936 there was a barium investigation revealing nothing more than visceroptosis and in 1943 there was a further examination, all with negative findings. Her doctor subsequently wrote in terms which did not substantiate her claims or those of the publication and gave his opinion that there was a large factor of functional exaggeration.

(D) The boy J. R. (Group 2) was according to the headlines 'permanently cured': 'Psychic healing succeeded when doctors failed', one of these read. He was 'given up by professors and doctors who examined him as a hopelessly incurable case. He was born paralysed in legs and arms, he was dumb and he had a distended stomach'. 'After fours years he received one treatment and the paralysis left him,' the account continued, 'the next morning he spoke and could run. . . . J. has now grown into a fine young man, leading a normal, happy life.'

In answer to my request, the hospital concerned reported that J. R. was an in-patient for two months in 1934, suffering from rickets, and was discharged 'improved'. From September 1934 to February 1935 he was treated for coeliac disease, chicken-pox and whooping cough and again discharged 'improved'. December 1948 to February 1949 he was suffering from Brodie's abscess of the ankle and was discharged with satisfactory results. There was no record of any other disability, temporary or permanent.

(E) Mr J. E. E. (Group 3) wrote to Harry Edwards in July 1953, 'In June 1952, after having been on your list of absent healing, I suddenly recovered the sight in my right eye which had been completely blind for over 50 years. It came as long sight and was pronounced by my specialist optician as perfect, and the healing as miraculous.' The specialist in ophthalmology is quoted as having reported '(1) Vision perfect; (2) eye clear, bright, in splendid condition; (3) absolutely no fear of deleterious effects, therefore no need whatever of worry.' It was also claimed that he was overheard to remark, 'It's miraculous.'

The ophthalmologist concerned was kind enough to write to me in October 1953, 'There is no miracle – [J. E. E.] was a case of spontaneous dislocation of lens which was cataractous. The lens dislocated back into his vitreous chamber, which is the old operation known as couching and is brought about by some violent exercise or sudden jerk – [a fact] generally forgotten when a miracle is under consideration. Although uncommon it is a well-known clinical entity.' There could in this case have been, I thought, functional blindness after the couching which was relieved by suggestion, the patient beginning to *see* after being encouraged to *look*.

(F) Mr R. B. (Group 3). A biopsy was carried out on this patient in June 1953, and a week later Mr B. was informed that he was suffering from cancer of the larynx calling for a major operation. Mr B. applied to Harry Edwards for direct healing, and during the interview his hoarse voice began to improve in quality and gain in volume. Then, on 21 July 1953, Mr B. was re-examined under an anaesthetic in hospital and informed that the pathologist's report was at variance with the previous one. Independent examination was arranged and a later report ran 'In all Mr B. has been examined by five throat specialists, one of whom is considered to be the greatest authority on cancer in this country. The two specialists who examined him after he had had direct healing from Mr Edwards both reported "no cancer now".' One of the surgeons wrote to me in December 1953: 'I doubt if anyone will give a definite reply ... my own belief is that it was pure fortunate coincidence that this man had a piece removed for biopsy and it happened to contain all of the carcinomatous tissues.'

Here I should perhaps break off to interpolate that a

biopsy is the removal for microscopic and other examinations of a piece of tissue suspected of being diseased. If the examination is carried out early enough it is possible that the removed specimen may contain *all* the diseased tissue, and, if there has been no infiltration into the surrounding structures, the biopsy is equivalent to operative removal. Surgeons and pathologists call this 'cure by biopsy'.

It happened that when my SPR paper was in the press I was carrying out a pilot research project in the Ear, Nose and Throat Department at St Bartholomew's Hospital, where at the invitation of the then senior surgeon of the department, Mr F. C. W. Capps, and in collaboration with Mr R. F. McNab Jones, I was having some success in treating by psychological methods patients who had failed to respond to the accepted mechanistic forms of treatment of vasomotor rhinitis. It was, therefore, quite by chance that I discovered that there had recently been in the department a patient whose history was almost identical with that of Mr R. B. except that he had been 'cured by biopsy' *without* the intervention of any form of faith healing. It appears now to be an accepted fact that such cures by biopsy are far from rare.

Returning to the body of my report, we come to :

(G) Dr O. (Group 4). In large headlines again, the press announced 'Doctor cured in three treatments.... My own profession would have kept me in hospital for weeks.' Four years previously, it was reported, Dr O. had acute pain in the lower back which was diagnosed as a 'slipped disc' and was relieved by a month's rest in bed. Two years later he again 'slipped the disc' following a fall. The symptoms were more severe than previously, the least movement causing acute pain, and an emergency appointment was arranged with a healer.

'Without undressing me or even taking off my coat,' the doctor reported, 'he ran his fingers down the centre of my back.... Reaching the spine he exclaimed. "Ah, here's the trouble, you'll be all right now." Beyond a slight swaying movement there was no attempt at manipulation of any kind. The acute pain left me at once and I got up and walked unassisted up some steps. The dull ache which was all that was left of the pain was cured by two subsequent treatments a few days later. This attack was incomparably more severe than the first. How should I have fared under orthodox surgical methods? I have often wondered.'

'Between these episodes' (continued the newspaper account) 'a sudden acute pain in the lower abdomen took Dr O. to a surgeon and two other doctors who diagnosed hernia, "small but definite". I walked with difficulty holding the rupture in with the fingers of my right hand. The surgeon said there could be no cure without operation and I asked for time to consider it. A friend, a scientist and a spirit healer in his spare time, treated me by laying on of hands under spirit influence. After four or five treatments the hernia completely disappeared – there has been no trouble since.'

My own comment on this case was that 'in the first illness described it is obvious that acute pain was the major factor, and neurologists and orthopaedic surgeons are familiar with the vagaries of the so-called "slipped disc" syndrome. The matter of the hernia would at first sight seem to afford incontrovertible evidence in favour of the healer. However, this phenomenon of spontaneous cure is known by surgeons to occur in the absence of therapeutic intervention'.

(H) I saw D. G. (Group 5) come on to the Festival Hall platform in September 1951 with severe kyphoscoliosis (curvature of the spine) and compensatory torticollis (twisting of the neck) which we were told were of long standing. Mr Edwards reduced the spinal curvature in his usual way by encouraging the patient to allow himself to move back and forth and sideways with the healer's hand supporting him. There appeared to be marked improvement in the spinal line, and a mild joke was created by the sight of the jacket which now possessed an un-filled sack where the deformed spine had previously lodged.

Meeting D. G. by chance after the demonstration it was pos-sible to talk in comparative privacy among the throng of people too busy to notice him. Commenting on the apparent improve-ment in his back and in the residual torticollis, I offered to reduce this and did so by placing one finger under his chin and encouraging him to allow his head to move into the normal position, at which point I said he would now remain well and left him. In the meantime I had taken particulars which en-abled me to ask for his hospital records. Regrettably many had been destroyed after the usual storage period, but there were records dating from 1946 from an orthopaedic hospital dis-closing a diagnosis of advanced spondylosis ankylo poetica: a Taylor's jacket and supportive physiotherapy had been recom-mended. In the middle of 1951 the patient had complained of pain and stiffness and 'would therefore appear to have de-veloped a further increase in flexion deformity in the spine in the course of the last year'.

Early in 1952 I renewed contact to inquire after his progress since the demonstration, only to find that the effects of Mr Edwards' treatment – and of my own – had lasted about three months, following which he had relapsed. A few weeks later he was admitted to hospital suffering from pulmonary tuber-culosis.

(1) Mrs G. M. L. (Group 5). A banner headline stated 'De-formity Melted Away'. 'Mrs G. M. L., who had no power in her hands for about ten years' (the story below it ran), 'and whose arms had been crippled with pain, was helped from the stage by a *Psychic News* reporter who writes, "She gripped my hand with the strength of a normal person."'

This lady, upon inquiry, wrote to me in these terms: 'I am sorry to tell you I am not cured of my complaint but, in fair-ness to Mr Edwards, had I followed his advice and continued with the psychic healing at my local spiritualist church I may have been by now. Also in fairness to Mr Edwards, after his treatment at the Pier Theatre, Hastings, I certainly did feel free of pain: *for the time* a new woman.'

(J) Miss E. W. (Group 6) was interviewed personally. This middle-aged lady had, at the age of three and a half years, 'been in splints for a year', during which time she had 'congestion of the lungs'. She also had 'spinal trouble' believed to be due to 'falls and tuberculosis'.

In June 1949 the patient fell down a steep staircase, and although only bruised she 'became more and more tired' and as the months passed the 'back ached where it was deformed'. Later she slipped and fell, following which she was unable to raise her leg: she 'dragged it along suffering agony' but did not attend her doctor as she was 'afraid of having to lie up again'. She went instead to a chiropractor who told her that 'three discs had slipped in the lumbar spine' and he 'thrust them into place'. He 'did not touch the dorsal spine, which was deformed, for fear of breaking it'.

After this she became worse and 'very bad at the walking', and experienced great difficulty in getting out of a chair or bed. Her own doctor referred her to a surgical specialist and she subsequently received physiotherapy, but the pain and disability increased until she could scarcely turn her head and 'it was awful in a car or bus'. Pain, disability and faulty gait persisted and in 1950 the patient contacted Mr Edwards and received absent healing.

After some months Miss W. 'did not get any worse' and was still reporting to the hospital for treatment. Pain and disability continued until mid-May when 'during the night I felt my neck being gripped and pulled and when I got up in the morning I found the top of the spine (which, as far back as I can remember, had protruded) had slipped into place and I was able to bend my neck from there which I had not been able to do'. There followed a journey to Mr Edwards who straightened the dorsal spine – 'which was certainly a miracle after being deformed for forty-two years'.

'I was able that day to throw away my stick and run into the house,' the patient reported in April 1952. 'I have no trouble in my balance and can now walk normally.' She added, however, 'I am hoping to get further benefit.' When I examined Miss W. in August 1952 she certainly appeared a reliable witness. She had visited a healer on the principle of trying any-thing – 'It couldn't do much harm', as she put it – and now had no symptoms except that 'the back does get a little tired'.

The surgeon originally responsible for treatment kindly agreed to see Miss W. again and report on her condition. His original reports revealed that she had attended the surgical out-patient department between 1949 and 1951. She had a dor-sal kyphosis (curvature of the spine), considered probably to be due to an old tubercular lesion of childhood. A possible diag-nosis of disseminated sclerosis had been rejected and the spas-ticity was thought to be associated with the spinal lesion. She received physiotherapy, a Taylor's brace, and some vitamin injections to relieve the neuritic pains. The report continued: 'One day after I had not seen her for some months she walked in and told me that she had been cured by a Christian Scien-tist. He had put his fingers on the prominence of her spine and she had had no symptoms since. I told her I was delighted that her symptoms had been relieved and she went away. I noted at the time that there was no obvious change in the physical state; the kyphosis was as marked as ever.'

After re-examining her in 1953 with the aid of the radiolo-gist, the same surgeon reported, 'It would seem ... that the physical state is ... as it was before she had her treatment, that is, the organic bone formation is actually the same. There is no doubt, however, that her movements are much better than they were before, due, I suspect, to the psychological im-provement.' Obviously there had been great functional im-provement in this case, but who shall say which kind of therapy or which therapist was responsible?

(k) Mrs L. W. (Group 6) had suffered from osteo-arthritis or rheumatism for fifteen years or more: during this time she was unable to walk, her knees being 'enormously swollen'. There was no response to treatment at various hospitals and clinics or at the hands of an osteopath. She was taken to Shere in January 1951 for treatment followed by absent healing. The first treatment provided immediate relief although con-siderable distress remained; but gradually the patient could lift her feet without pain.

Describing the treatment by Mr Edwards, Mrs W. commented that he had lifted her leg right up without pain, which she 'couldn't possibly have stood if a hospital doctor [or she herself] had attempted it'. She continued to receive treatment from a healer 'for fear of slipping back'. The patient commented that during the several weeks of waiting for her healing interview she received absent healing. One night she was awakened by the feeling that the door had opened and a presence was beside her bed: she felt herself turned over and there was something like a murmur of voices in the room. She fancied herself 'a little easier' the next day.

The hospital concerned reported that this lady had, since 1948, been attending for treatment of a non-toxic goitre. In addition she had been treated from November 1950 to June 1951 for benign hypertension, obesity, and osteo-arthritis of both knees – the latter being checked by X-ray examinations. There was 'considerable symptomatic improvement' when she was last seen. Her physician wrote in October 1952 to say '... she seems to have improved subjectively a good deal since the laying on of hands of her spirit healer [but] we can find little change since before this operation ... the angles of movement are about the same as they were at that time. I think this is primarily degenerative joint disease plus psychogenic pain – a field which is peculiarly susceptible to cure by spirit healers.'

(L) M. R. (Group 8), a boy aged 9, was suffering from pseudo-hypertrophic muscular dystrophy. When I examined him in December 1951 he was free of spinal deformity. He later visited Mr Edwards who told him he 'would get better and that he had straightened his back'. The family general practitioner wrote in February 1953, 'I am sorry to report that in my opinion the condition is very definitely worse.'

Such were the twelve cases – just over one eighth of the total which I had investigated by 1954 – which I thought typical of the way in which what at first sight appears a striking, remarkable or even miraculous cure becomes much less noteworthy when subjected to dispassionate inquiry and normal medical 'follow-up'. I do not quote this material here, however, as a corrective to the unvaryingly rosy pictures presented by *Psychic News* and the like so much as to illustrate the type of evidence which brought me to the conclusion that, whatever else I might have discovered, I had not come within hailing distance of a single example of the type of 'miracle cure' which I was seeking.

I did, however, continue to open up new lines of approach. In May 1955, I got in touch with the secretary of the Churches' Fellowship for Psychical Study – the body, referred to earlier, which believed at its foundation that it would gather evidence for the reality of paranormal healing within six months and which (according to a press report) had by then begun to assess its findings.

The secretary replied saying that he did not know much about the subject but would like to come and see me. We had a pleasant meeting, though I think I went out of favour when I showed no great interest in other types of Spiritualist phenomena. But he promised to help me with my search for facts, and referred me to the chairman of the sub-committee which was actually carrying out the research. I then wrote to the chairman, asking if he could give me what I needed. He replied, saying that it was not really he who was concerned but yet another party who was conducting the experiments, assessing the facts and forming the conclusions. So I wrote to the third of this chain of informants – and got no reply.

In due course, however, the Churches' Fellowship published the results of its own 'experiment in healing': with the co-operation of fourteen physicians it had tried the effect of absent healing on 140 sufferers from such diseases as spasticity, rheumatism and mental retardation. Sixty-six of these were reported to show a 'definite improvement' and there were two 'complete cures'. It was not clear, however, that concurrent orthodox medical treatment was excluded.

Also belonging to this period was a distressingly memorable meeting between the late W. J. Macmillan (whose book on healing I had reviewed and found factually unsatisfying), a general practitioner who had himself been healed by Harry Edwards, Dr Weatherhead, several other interested students of this problem, and myself. Mr Macmillan 'the reluctant healer', however, announced that he was prepared neither to talk nor to answer questions; and Dr Weatherhead was prepared to do both but not on the subject of healing! Somebody else left to catch a train, and so what might have been a really useful meeting petered out amid general philosophical exchanges.

The degree of interest in certain subjects often seems to run in cycles in which a personal involvement coincides with a national or even a world-wide one. Certainly the period of 1954–5, which witnessed the deliberations of the Archbishops' Commission, the appearance of Harry Edwards in the limelight of press and television, the publication of the Churches' Fellowship report, the conferences of the Parapsychology Foundation and my own independent labours, marked a peak in the curve. In the second half of the 1950s, by contrast, public interest in faith cures died away somewhat, as is reflected even in the publication dates of the works which I quote in a later bibliography.

This was perhaps partly due to the amount of quite serious interest then being paid to radiaesthesia. This engaged my own attention for a while, and at one stage I considered including a chapter here on my investigations of the work of Mr de la Warr and others. I decided against this, though, on the grounds that though radiaesthesic diagnosis and healing might well be relevant to considerations of suggestibility it was much less so to the world in which the faith healers operated. In this context, the 'black box' proved a red herring. It is enough to add that I was unable to obtain from Mr de la Warr any of the data upon which he based his claims. In my view, and in that of the late Lord Horder with whom I compared impressions, this work warranted no further study. An authoritative academic inquiry in Belgium had already found a similar lack of evidence to support the thesis of radiaesthesia.

All the time, however, I continued – however slowly – on my main line of research. At one stage, for instance, I got in touch with Mr George Rogers, the then Labour MP for Kensington North, whose wife was a faith healer and who was himself a firm believer in her powers. Perhaps it was unfortunate that my first approach to him, at which I asked for a case history backed by proper records of just one patient who had been either markedly improved or cured of a measurable organic disease by his wife's activities alone, coincided with a general election at which he had to fight a marginal seat, but he accepted my 'kind offer in principle' and we left it that he would get in touch with me as soon as he was free to do so. Since then I have heard nothing.

Furthermore, my dialogue with Harry Edwards continued. We spent a great deal of time, for instance, over the case of a 'Major M.', who believed that he had been cured of severe fractures and wounds by Mr Edwards: the pain and disability at least were said to have vanished, though the anatomical destruction had not been made good. Major M. stated that there were X-ray negatives and consultants' records to confirm his story.

At one stage Mr Edwards reproached me with not having taken up this case with sufficient fervour. What actually happened, however, was that when I wrote to Major M. asking where I could find the medical records he replied that, as I was not in his view a believer, he felt that

I was not a suitable person to have access to them. It is interesting that Major M. had talked to me at great length about a psychic experience which, he claimed, had led to his being able to get his men through enemy lines during World War II: this incident was by its nature not susceptible to documentary confirmation.

Still more promising seemed a case which was brought to my notice in the mid-sixties as 'The Case of the Year'. This turned out to lead to a typical illustration of the difficulties which arise in the dialogue between physician and faith healer, and so I will start by quoting from the official medical history of the patient, dated November 1965, which was sent to me by Mr Edwards.

The patient [this ran] is Mr S., aged 71, diagnosed as suffering from cervical spondylosis with vertebrobasilar insufficiency. [Spinal disease with circulatory impairment.]

The patient has been known for at least ten years to suffer from severe spondylosis.

In May 1965 he was seized with a further attack of acute stiff neck, this time accompanied by dysphagia [difficulty in swallowing] and later by trismus [lockjaw], diplopia [double vision] and retention of urine.

When first seen the muscular spasm around the neck and the trismus were sufficiently severe to suggest the possibility of tetanus and [Mr S.] was treated with anti-tetanus serum without result. Neck traction gave a brief period of relief, but the dysphagia rapidly became so bad that even tube feeding was impossible and the patient had attacks of laryngeal spasm.

On the fourth day of his illness a tracheotomy [placing a tube into the windpipe] was performed by Dr B., and the patient was transferred to the Intensive Care Unit.

Here all his symptoms gradually subsided over about two weeks and he finally made a complete recovery.

The patient himself attributes his remarkable recovery from what was an extremely anxious and frightening illness to spiritual healing.

168

In his accompanying letter to me, Mr Edwards wrote:

A doctor who attended the patient called it 'The Case of the Year'. The patient was invited to attend a doctors' conference at the Royal East Sussex Hospital. A copy of the above medical history was provided for each doctor. He was asked many questions and the doctors wanted to [know] what was this 'spiritual healing'. He told them how different he was after seeing Mr A. T. Huxford (a spiritual healer and member of the National Federation of Spiritual Healers), and that he was still seeing him once a week.

Spondylosis is the fusing up of the spinal bones – in this case in the neck. It was so severe that he could not move his jaws or swallow any food. Medically this is a totally incurable condition, often leading to death. His recovery was so 'remarkable', to use the official word, that the man was used as an exhibition case.

This is one of the few occasions when we [that is, Mr Edwards' Federation] are able to provide an official medical history to substantiate a spiritual healing. It is a testimony to the work of healing that carries on day by day throughout the land.

The day after receiving this material – the 12 January 1966 – I wrote to the surgeon concerned, Mr E. W. Bintcliffe of the Royal East Sussex Hospital, asking for more information and, if possible, a sight of the case notes. He replied promptly saying that Dr R. E. Irvine had been responsible for Mr S. during his stay in the hospital and would be able to give me more details. However, Mr Bintcliffe ended his letter 'I did see the patient during the acute stage of his illness and he was suffering from cervical spondylosis with some unusual features. He has certainly made a remarkable recovery and I am sure this is due to the excellent work which was done in the Intensive Care Unit of this hospital.'

Dr Irvine wrote to me shortly afterwards, adding:

As far as Mr S.'s basic cervical spondylosis is concerned there has certainly been no change. The remarkable fact about his recovery was, as you surmised, the way he recovered from the trismus and laryngeal spasm. I quite agree with you that in this the work of the Intensive Care Unit was a major factor. I do, however, think that the spiritual healer, who I never met or watched at work, did in some way help Mr S. to relax and to face a short but very distressing illness more calmly, and in this way he probably made a useful contribution. I was impressed by the more co-operative attitude of both the patient and his wife when I allowed their request for the patient to be seen by the spiritual healer.

Later I talked with Mr Edwards briefly about Mr S., and he wrote to me on 18 March, saying, 'Since I spoke to you on this last Saturday, I have made inquiries and been informed that NO special treatment was given in the Intensive Care Unit. [Mr S.] only received nursing.

'Let me recap,' continued Harry Edwards:

The patient suffered from severe cervical spondylosis for ten years, which developed into trismus and dysphagia. His condition deteriorated so much that even tube feeding was impossible with laryngeal spasms, when after receiving tracheotomy he was then sent to the Intensive Care Unit where he was 'nursed' until he was expected to die.

Please note that it was when the man was transferred to the Intensive Care Unit that spiritual healing entered into the picture, with the patient receiving healing from a local healer. Only then came the change, and the official medical history reports 'all his symptoms gradually subsided over about two weeks and he made a complete recovery.'

The doctors headed their official summary with the heading: 'The Case of the Year'. The recovery could not be medically anticipated: it was so super-normal that he was presented as an exhibition case before a panel of doctors.

If you cannot accept this case as proven ... I suggest you should give up your inquiry, for I can see no reason for further co-operation between us.

It seems to me that your method of judging spiritual healing is unreasonable. If a patient has received medical attention, you attribute the recovery, no matter how remarkable, to this and not to spiritual healing. Obviously, any patient condemned to being 'incurable' must have received medical treatment.

The alternative is, that to prove spiritual healing to satisfy you, the sick person must not have received medical attention at any time. In this event there could be no medical diagnosis or history ... and then you would dispute the healing because there could not have been a proper diagnosis.

It's a case of 'heads I win, tails you lose'.

I have quoted Mr Edwards at length, and would like to stress that I sympathize with his point of view and realize how frustrating my interpretation of the history must appear to him. When I replied I tried to pinpoint our basic difference and said, 'The thesis which developed as I went on studying the problem boiled down to the need to establish that a measurable organic disease could be improved or cured by spiritual healing when medical treatment had either failed or was not being applied, and these criteria do not seem to me to be satisfied by Mr S.'s case.'

The struggle for agreement about definitions and criteria continued between us, and is summarized in my letter to Dr Irvine of the 9 May 1966, which I quote in full:

I wonder if I could bother you to comment on the present position in my discussion with Mr Edwards, the faith healer. I have said 'The Intensive Care Unit has a wide-ranging staff of surgeons, physicians, anaesthetists and so on capable of dealing with critical illness until the patient is in a state fit for *normal* nursing and treatment', and I added to Mr Edwards 'You say that in Mr S.'s case incurability was established. This is not the case, since he was admitted to an Intensive Care Unit firstly to save his life and from that point to get on with rehabilitation'.

Mr Edwards replies [I continued to Dr Irvine] 'Why do you persistently ignore the truth that Mr S. did NOT receive any specialized treatment in the ICU? This man had chronic spondylosis, developed over a period of ten years, culminating in lockjaw and paralysis of the throat. He could not even take fluids. A tracheotomy had to be performed to save his life. He was transferred to the ICU for nursing, the hospital doctors being unable to do anything more for him. In the ICU, I repeat again, the only treatment he received was being fed through the tube and general nursing. He did not (I repeat NOT) receive any specialized treatment as you suggest he did. You are supposed to be investigating spiritual healings and you base your refutation of this case solely on the ground that he was sent to an ICU. Right! Then, if you have investigated, tell me *WHAT* intensive specialized treatment Mr S. received. This is your obvious ground for investigation. I do not think you have bothered to do this so far; but I have, and he only received general nursing. Have you ever heard of a patient suffering from similar conditions who recovered with medical treatment?'

Dr Irvine replied to me:

I would have thought that your description of the Intensive Care Unit was entirely accurate, and I would agree with every word.

It seems to me that if Mr S. had not been able to continue to breathe through his tracheotomy, and be fed through the stomach tube, he would not have lived long enough to benefit from the improvement in his cerebrovascular disease.

What improved his cerebral circulation and restored his power to swallow and move his jaws, I cannot say.

And so once more we reached an impasse. Mr Edwards was obviously sincere in believing that this case met his criteria of a 'miracle cure'. But from the point of view of medical pathology it is an unusual case but certainly not one which demands the positing of completely novel forces of nature.

Earlier on the idea had formed itself that it ought to be of value to approach the homes for incurables. My aim here was admittedly slightly different, inasmuch as, with my former attacks on the problem so often seeming to lead only to 'the department of dead ends', it seemed possible that through these one could design a controlled experiment in healing. One of these homes – at Putney – had replied without delay that 'psychic healing has no place in this institution': this meant that it had no interest in a course of action (e.g., the laying on of hands by Harry Edwards or prayer by Christopher Woodard) which could have no ill effects on its patients and might well produce favourable ones – and which might have yielded valuable information too. The other hospital, at Streatham, took nearly four months to decide against proceeding with the proposition.

Now, in July 1966, I wrote again to the medical officer of the Putney home asking, 'Firstly, is there any record of any of your patients ever being discharged completely relieved of the illness for which admitted; and, secondly, is there any evidence that such relief was associated at all with the activities of a faith healer by direct communication, laying on of hands, absent healing and so on?' To this he replied, 'None of my patients has ever been discharged completely relieved of the illness for which they were admitted; and this answers your second question.'

My latest step in an inquiry which still continues whenever time and opportunity present was to write to Mr J. Bernard Hutton, who had been healed and had written the story of his healer. I asked him in particular whether it would be possible for me to see any of the medical records which he had referred to in print. I received no reply; but when three weeks later Mr Hutton was addressing a meeting (at which I also contributed some comments on his book) he apologized for his lack of response. Though he made no offer of medical records he did promise to let me have his hospital reference number so that I could follow up his case for myself. I am still waiting to receive this, but it seems clear that neither his own case history nor that of any other patient he mentions in his book is amenable to disciplined examination. The authorities he quotes are certainly less than satisfactory; for one died after attending the healer, another was a dentist who removed his name from the dental register, and a third had no relevant records of the patient concerned. Once more I seemed to have reached a dead end.

And meanwhile, in March 1966, Harry Edwards had again taken the stage – this time at the Central Hall, Westminster, where he participated in what had come to be known by the curious term 'teach-in'. In fact (as viewed from any impartial standpoint) this festival can have done little to increase public confidence in faith healers; for though we heard statements of every point of view from the Quaker to the Roman Catholic on the Christian front and from the Spiritualist to the Buddhist among the rest, no one doctrine seemed to emerge on which even the enthusiasts were in agreement. All that was clear was that, once more, public interest was demanding an answer to the question which has run through this book: Does faith healing work?

I began this chapter with a quotation relating to Mrs Eddy: perhaps I may finish it in the same fashion. In his outspoken attack on 'Mother Mary', Mark Twain remarked that the whole structure of 'Christian Science' was created 'without ever presenting anything which may rightfully be called by the strong name of evidence'. The last chapter of this book, limited in its scope and negative in its findings as it may have been, is at least composed of material which merits that 'strong name'.

# Conclusion

THIS search for the truth concerning faith healing has contained – as perhaps any scientific investigation must – a number of direct clashes of evidence: but in general my problem has been the lack of evidence. This final note must hence be regarded only as a survey of work to date and most certainly not as a final solution.

Broadly, it is possible to take five attitudes towards purported faith cures. One can ignore the entire subject, a course which would seem inadvisable for mankind as a whole and one which physicians in particular would find hard to justify. One can deny that there are any phenomena worthy of critical attention, a view which would perhaps be reasonable were faith cures as rare as successful alchemists. One can uncritically accept that paranormal forces intervene in the affairs of human health, or one can equally uncritically assume that any and every example of the healer's art will be found explicable through considerations of suggestion, spontaneous remission, misplaced records and the like. And finally one can set oneself to take at least the first step towards an evaluation of these puzzling phenomena.

This last was the course which I adopted when, after a review of the material available, I narrowed my quest to the search for a handful of cases – or perhaps only a single case – in which the intervention of a faith healer had led to an irrefutable cure. This must have been a cure, not in the vague sense of a patient's 'feeling better' or even in that a progressive disease had been limited, but in the sense that, as a result of the healer's work alone, a demonstrable pathological state had been entirely eliminated.

To those who have read this book it will be clear that in that search I have been unsuccessful. After nearly twenty years of work I have yet to find one 'miracle cure'; and without that (or, alternatively, massive statistics which others must provide) I cannot be convinced of the efficacy of what is commonly termed faith healing. But my mind is certainly not closed to new evidence, and I remain interested in examining any claims of unorthodox cures with hard facts to support them.

Many would feel that the problem of faith healing can still best be summarized by some words contained in the report of the Archbishop of Canterbury's committee of 1920 which was published over forty-six years ago. 'Our committee' (this read) 'has found no evidence of any cases of healing which [could] not be paralleled by similar cures wrought by psychotherapy without religion, and by instances of spontaneous healing which often occur even in the gravest cases in ordinary medical practice.' And some thirty years afterwards the BMA committee which advised the later church commission reached similar findings:

We can find no evidence [they concluded] that there is any type of illness cured by 'spiritual healing' alone which could not have been cured by medical treatment. . . . We find that, whilst patients suffering from psychogenic disorders may be 'cured' by various methods of spiritual healing, just as they are by methods of suggestion and other forms of psychological treatment employed by doctors [there is] no evidence that organic diseases are cured solely by such means. The evidence suggests that many such cases claimed to be cured are likely to be either instances of wrong diagnosis, wrong prognosis, remission or . . . spontaneous cure.

These are authoritative statements, against which I have found nothing to weigh except shadowy claims and cases which refuse to assume substance. Yet the shadow remains a massive one; and I certainly do not feel that I have reached the end of a road. Rather, I find myself in agreement with the Very Rev. George Johnstone Jeffrey who, when considering this subject, paraphrased the words of the statesman and scholar Augustine Birrell.

The only man with a right to the last word on faith healing, Jeffrey suggested, would be the last man on earth.

# Postscript

BY PROFESSOR W. LINFORD REES

*Professor of psychiatry and Physician in charge of the
Department of Psychological Medicine, St Bartholomew's Hospital.
Member of the Medical Research Council.*

IN this book, Dr Rose has shown that healing by faith as well as healing by magic can be traced to the dawn of civilization. Ancient medicine functioned on the belief that diseases were caused by demons. Early Assyrian tablets described methods of curing illness by driving out demons with magic, charms, incantations and rituals. In the famous temples of healing of Aesculapius in Greece, religious methods of healing were employed: patients came long distances, offered valuable gifts to influence the gods favourably, spent some nights taking part in public prayers and exhortations, and before the statue of a god were given advice in the form of oracles and prophetic dreams.

Throughout the Middle Ages the tradition of magic persisted, but in addition shrines were visited and saints invoked to cure particular diseases. By the authority of their names and the influence of their words, pious persons too would sometimes produce remarkable cures which were regarded as the outcome of divine intervention. Dr Rose has traced the development of healing from these early forms down to the work of the 'animal magnetizers' or hypnotists and has gone on to deal with the work of the Spiritualists, 'Christian Scientists', and other religious and quasi-religious bodies who specialize in such treatment today.

There is evidence that a significant element in most

forms of magical and religious healing is the influence of suggestion as a therapeutic agent. In some forms of religious activity the effect of suggestion is extremely powerful, especially if a state of excitation is aroused: this is followed by a state of collapse during which suggestion has a very marked effect, as is mentioned in a work by Dr Sargant to which Dr Rose has referred. Suggestion can also produce beneficial effects in illness of mental origin – for example in functional and certain psychosomatic disorders – and may alleviate the distress of disease without influencing the underlying pathology.

Although faith may require no evidence, most people need to have some evidence if they are to accept the claims made by faith healers. In what is perhaps the most valuable part of this book, Dr Rose has laid down precise criteria with regard to the claims for faith healing, and has shown how evidence in this field can be carefully marshalled and subjected to cool and critical appraisal. In so doing, I believe, he has filled a long-felt need.

W.L.R.

# Works Consulted

The bibliography of faith healing is, as mentioned in the introduction, a very considerable one even when restricted to bound works published in English in the present century. A glance at Dwyer (see below) will confirm this fact; and many useful books have been published since this valuable abstract was compiled. Accordingly, I have suggested in list A below only a selection of some sixty books representative of various approaches to the subject: many of these contain their own extensive bibiographies.

Most of the works included in this first list are general or religious in their approach. List B is concerned first with periodicals and then with pamphlets, the majority of the former being medical in their approach.

## A

Balint, M., *The Doctor, His Patient and the Illness*, Pitman, 1957.

Barbanell, M., *I Hear a Voice*, Spiritualist Press, 1962. Etc.

Bellak, L., *Psychology of Physical Illness*, Churchill, 1953.

Bender, H., *Faith Healing and Parapsychology in Magic and Miracle in the Act of Healing*, Stuttgart, 1959. Etc.

Bramwell, J. M., *Hypnotism*, New York, 1956.

Brown, W., *Mind, Medicine and Metaphysics*, Oxford University Press, 1936.

Colinon, M., *The Healers*, Paris, 1957.

Cummins, G., *et al.*, *Perceptive Healing*, Rider, 1945.

Dawson, G. G., *Healing, Pagan and Christian*, Society for Promoting Christian Knowledge, 1935.

Dearmer, P., *Body and Soul*, Pitman, 1909.

Desmond, A. K., *The Gift of Healing*, Spiritualist Press, 1943.

Dunbar, H. F., *Psychosomatic Diagnosis*, New York, 1943.

Eddy, M. B. G., *Science and Health*, Boston, 1875.

Edwards, H., *The Power of Spiritual Healing*, Herbert Jenkins, 1963. Etc.

Ehrenwald, J. (Ed.), *From Medicine Man to Freud*, New York, 1956.

Entralgo, P. L., *Mind and Body*, Harvill Press, 1955.

Frayling, M., *The Quest for Spiritual Healing*, Rider, 1951.

## WORKS CONSULTED

Frazer, J. G., *The Golden Bough*, Macmillan, 1922.

Frost, E., *Christian Healing*, A. R. Mowbray, 1940.

Garlick, P. L., *The Wholeness of Man*, Church Missionary Society, 1943.

Gregory, M., *Psychotherapy, Scientific and Religious*, Macmillan, 1939.

Grinker, R. R., *Psychosomatic Research*, New York, 1953.

Haggard, H. W., *Devils, Drugs and Doctors*, Heinemann, n. d.

Hutchison, H., *The Church and Spiritual Healing*, Rider, 1955.

Hutton, J. B., *Healing Hands*, W. H. Allen, 1966.

Ikin, A. G., *New Concepts of Healing*, Hodder, 1955.

Inglis, B., *Fringe Medicine*, Faber, 1964.

Kelly, G. A., *The Psychology of Personal Constructs*, New York, 1955.

Kerin, D., *Fulfilling*, Wessex Press, 1952.

Leuret, F., *et al.*, *Modern Miraculous Cures*, Peter Davies, 1957.

Mackenna, R. M. B., *Modern Trends in Dermatology*, Butterworth, 1954.

Macmillan, W. J., *The Reluctant Healer*, Gollancz, 1952.

Maher, B. (Ed.), *Progress in Experimental Personality Research*, Academic Press, 1964.

Major, R. H., *Faiths that Healed*, New York, 1940.

Malinowski, B. K., *Magic, Science and Religion*, Free Press, 1949.

Martin, B., *The Healing Ministry in the Church*, Lutterworth, 1960.

Miller, P., *Born to Heal*, Spiritualist Press, 1948.

Murray, G., *Frontiers of Healing*, Max Parrish, 1958. Etc.

Murray, J. B., *Some Common Psychosomatic Manifestations*, Oxford University Press, 1951.

Needham, J. (Ed.), *Science, Religion and Reality*, Sheldon, 1925.

Oursler, W., *The Healing Power of Faith*, The World's Work, 1958.

Peddie, J. C., *The Forgotten Talent*, Oldbourne, 1961.

Pettigrew, T. J., *Superstitions Connected with the History and Practice of Medicine and Surgery*, John Churchill, 1844.

Pitts, J., *Divine Healing – Fact and Fiction*, Arthur James, 1962.

Racanelli, F., *Gift of Healing*, Munich, 1953.

Rivers, W. H. R., *Medicine, Magic and Religion*, Routledge, 1924.

Roberts, C. E. B., *The Truth about Spiritualism*, Eyre & Spottiswoode, 1932.

Sargant, W., *Battle for the Mind*, Heinemann, 1957.

Scherzer, C. J., *The Church and Healing*, Philadelphia, 1950.

Stokvis, B., *et al.*, *Suggestion*, Basle, 1961.

Tenhaeff, W. H. C., *Paranormal Healing Powers*, Olten, 1957.

Thompson, C. J. S., *Magic and Healing*, Rider, 1947.

Thouless, R. H., *Experimental Psychical Research*, Pelican, 1963.

Weatherhead, L. D., *Psychology, Religion and Healing*, Hodder, 1951.

Weiss, E., *et al.*, *Psychosomatic Medicine*, Saunders, 1949.

West, D. J., *Eleven Lourdes Miracles*, Duckworth, 1957. Etc.

Wickland, C. A., *Thirty Years among the Dead*, Los Angeles, 1925.

Wood, W. (Ed.), *New Horizons of Healing*, Arthur James, 1954.

Woodard, C., *A Doctor Heals by Faith*, Max Parrish, 1953. Etc.

Woods, B. E., *The Healing Ministry*, Rider, 1961.

Wyman, F. L., *Divine Healing*, Bannisdale, 1951.

Zweig, S., *Mental Healers*, Cassell, 1933.


B

Balint, M., 'Notes on Parapsychology', etc., *International Journal of Psychoanalysis*, 36, Pt I, 1955.

Bessemans, A., *et al.*, 'Scientific Inquest on So-called Medical Radiaesthesia', *Bruxelles-Medical*, 28 February 1948.

Edwards, J. Griffith, 'Role Playing Theory versus Clinical Psychiatry', *International Journal of Psychiatry*, Vol. III, No. 3, March 1967.

Flind, J., *et al.*, 'The Psychogenic Basis of ... Rheumatic Pains', *Quarterly Journal of Medicine*, 14, 1945.

Gould, J. G., '... Autohypnosis ...', *Journal of Mental Science*, 99, 273, 1953.

Knowles, F. W., 'Some Investigations into Psychic Healing', *Journal of the Institute of the American Society of Psychical Research*, 48, 1 January 1954.

Lasagna, L., *et al.*, 'A Study of the Placebo Response', *American Journal of Medicine*, 16, 1954.

Pepper, O. H. P., 'A Note on the Placebo', *American Journal of Pharmacy*, 117, 1945.

Reading, P., *et al.*, 'Results of Treatment of Chronic Vasomotor Rhinitis', *British Medical Journal*, March 1954.

Rehder, H., 'Miracle Cures', *Hippokrates*, Vol. 26, pp. 577–80.

Rose, L., 'Some Aspects of Paranormal Healing', *British Medical Journal*, December 1954.
'Some Aspects of Paranormal Healing', *Journal of the Society for Psychical Research*, September 1955.

Sarbin, T. R., 'The Concept of Role-Taking', *Sociometry*, VI, 1943.
*et al.*, 'Contributions to Role-Taking Theory', *Journal of Abnormal and Social Psychology*, 47, 117, 1952.

# WORKS CONSULTED

Strauss, E. B., 'Reason and Unreason in Psychological Medicine', *Lancet*, 2, 1, 49, 1952.

Thouless, R. H., 'Experiment in Spiritual Healing', *Newsletter of the Parapsychological Foundation*, Vol. II, No. 2, 1955.

West, D. J., *et al.*, *Tomorrow*, Vol. III, No. 3, 1955.

Wittkower, E., *et al.*, 'Effort Syndrome', *Lancet*, 531, 1941.

Wood, P., 'Differential Diagnosis of "Da Costa's" Syndrome', *Proceedings of the Royal Society of Medicine*, 34, 543. Etc.

Woolfe, T. P., 'Emotions and Organic Heart Disease', *American Journal of Psychology*, 93, 681, 1936. Etc.


*The Church's Ministry of Healing*. The Church Information Board, 1958.

*Divine Healing and Co-operation between Doctors and Clergy*, British Medical Association, 1956.

*The Ministry of Healing*, Society for Promoting Christian Knowledge, 1923.

*Spiritual Healing in the United States and Great Britain*. A bibliography assembled by W. W. Dwyer, New Jersey, 1953.

# Index

Absent Healing, 48, 63, 65
Adelphi, London, 'Temple of Health' in, 57
Aesculapius, 24, 28, 30, 178
Aestheric continuum, Mesmer's concept of, 53
Agatha, St, 34
Agues, 42
Albert, St, 39
Alexander, Franz, 120
Alexandria, mystical sects of, 30
Allopathic medication, 13
Alstead, Professor, 143
Ambrose of Milan, 30
Andrew, Brother. See Bessette, Alfred
Anglicans. See Church of England
Animal magnetism. See Magnetism
Animals, healing ministrations to, 30, 79, 98
Anne, Queen, 38
Anointing with oil, 88, 100
Anthony, St, 34
Anthroposophy, Rudolph Steiner's, 62
Antioch, Council of, 32
Aphraates, St, 30
Aphrodisiacs, 37
Apollonia, St, 34
Apollonius of Tyana, 25
Apothecary, 33
Archbishops' Commission on healing, 12, 108–9, 166
Aristotelian theory of elements, 39
Assyrian cures, 178
Astrology, 38–9, 113
Augustine, St, 30
Auto-suggestion, 132–3
Avicenna, 133

Baal Shem-Tov, 58
Back, diseases of the, 34
Balint, Dr Michael, 90, 135
Baltimore, 76
Bamberg, 48
Baptists, 97
Barber, 33
Barnabas, St, 29
Barnes, G. O., 79
Barrett, Elizabeth, 71
Barrett, Sir William, 71, 117
Bath, magic springs at, 33
Bavaria, 47
Beard, Rebecca, 75
Beauraing, Belgium, healing shrine at, 92
Becket, St Thomas à, 34
Beds. See Healing beds
Bedside manner, 122
Beesley, Ronald, 76
Belgium, 92, 167
Belloc, Hilaire, quoted, 136
Bender, Professor Hans, 144
Benedict XIV, Pope, 90
Benign tumours, 120
Bernadette, St, 93
Bernard of Clairvaux, St, 35
Bernheim, Hippolite, 129
Besant, Annie, 67
Bessette, Alfred (Brother Andrew), 74
Bethsea centres, 72
Beuno, St, 11, 114
Bi-metallic 'tractors', 57
Binger, Carl, 120
Bintcliffe, E. W., 169
Biopsy, 158–9
Birrell, Augustine, 177
Blaise, St, 34, 91
Blavatsky, Mme, 66–7

Bleeding, 33

Blindness, 27, 29, 42, 53, 60, 105, 115, 157-8

Blue baby condition, 82

Blumhardt, Pastor Johann, 98

Boggs, Professor Wade, quoted, 117-18

Bone diseases, 115

Bosco, St John, 91

Bostock, Bridget, 43-4

Boyle, Robert, 42

Braid, James, 56, 128-9

'Brain washing', 119

Brazil, 74

Breasts, 34

Bright's disease, 77

British Medical Association, 109, 129, 155, 176

*British Medical Journal*, 151, 155

Brodie's abscess of the ankle, 157

Broken bones, 76

Bronchial disorders, 120

Browning, Oscar, 71

Buddha, 26

Buddhism, 174

*Bureau des Constatations. See* Lourdes

Burgarde, St, 34

Burrswood, Kent, church of Christ the Healer at, 105

Burt, Sir Cyril, quoted, 20

Cabrini, St Frances. *See* Frances Cabrini, St

Cagliostro, Count, 58

Calvin, John, 97

Calvinism, 40

Cambridge, 25

Camps Farthest Out, 75

Canada, 18

Cancer, 34, 75, 76, 84, 120, 128, 158

Canterbury, Archbishop of, 105, 107, 108, 176; sets up Committee in 1920 on Healing Ministry, 108, 176

Capps, F. C. W., 159

Caradoc, Prince, 11

Card-telling, Dr Rhine's, 149

Carrel, Alexis, 93

Catherine of Siena, St, 34

Catholic church. *See* Roman Catholic church

Cattle, cure for diseased, 33

Cayce, Edward, 77-8

Cerebro-spinal meningitis, 81

Cervical erosion, 157

Charcot, J. M., 129

Charles I, 37

Charles II, 37

Chesterfield, Earl of, 57

Chichester, Sir Francis, 106

China school of paranormal therapy in, 80

Chiropractice, 64

Cholera, 97

Christ. *See* Jesus of Nazareth

Christian Science, 14, 73, 96, 101, 116, 117-18, 120, 123, 142, 174, 178; founded by Mrs Eddy, 64; its shortcomings, 66-9

*Christian Science Monitor, The*, 67

Chrysostom, St, 30

Church of England: revival of healing by Hickson, 102-3; centres of healing, 103-4; corporate curative movements, 104-5; nursing homes, 105; and ecumenical bodies, 105-6; and individual enthusiasts, 106; and miracles, 107; investigations into healing, 107-9, 145, 155, 166, 176

Church of Scotland. *See* Scotland

Churches' Council of Healing, 105

Churches' Fellowship for Psychical Study, 105-6, 165, 166

*Church's Ministry of Healing, The* (report), 12, 108

City Temple, London, 101

Clairvoyance, 70

Clark, Glenn, 75
Clovis, King, 36
Cobb, Rev. Howard, 103
Coins, blessing of, 37
Colic, 35–6
Colinon, Maurice, 80, 127–8
Colour-magic, 34
Compensatory torticollis, 160
Congregationalists, 97
Constantine the Great, 31
Conversion hysteria, 121
Convulsions, 53
Copper amulets, to guard against
  rheumatism, 34
Coronary thrombosis, 120
Cosmas, St, 34
Coué, Émile, 133–4
Cramp, 37
Cromwell, Oliver, 37
Crookes, Sir William, 71
Crowhurst, Sussex, Home of
  Healing at, 103
Cullen, William, 119
Cupping, 33
Curé d'Ars. See Vianney, St
  John

Damian, St, 34
d'Angelo, Achille, 57, 80, 143
Davis, Andrew Jackson, 60
Davy, Sir Humphry, 133
Day, Rev. Dr Albert, 76, 99, 143
Dead brought to life. See Resur-
  rection of the dead
Deafness, 115
Deformities, 114
De la Warr, Mr, 166–7
Delboeuf, quoted, 122
Descartes, 39
Devil, may cure for his own
  ends, 92. See also Diabolical
  possession
Diabetes, 120
Diabolical possession, 44, 45, 82.
  See also Exorcism
Diagnosis, 23, 75, 78; mistaken,
  137

Digby, Sir Kenelm, 39
Dingwall, Dr Eric, quoted, 154
Dissenting sects, 96–103
Divine, Father, 75
Divine healing, the Archbishops'
  Commission's comment on the
  term, 12, 13
Divine Healing Mission, Hick-
  son's, 103
'Divinity' movement, 78
Dorsal kyphosis, 163
Dorset, 33
Double-blind method of random-
  ization, 134
Dowie, J. A., 79
Doyle, Sir Arthur Conan, 71
Dropsy, 43
Drugs, 65, 134
Dysentery, 29

Ecclesiasticus, 26
Ectoplasm, 73, 78
Ecumenical bodies, 105–6
Eddy, Mrs Mary Baker, 63–9, 115,
  116, 141, 174
Edward the Confessor, 36
Edwards, Dr Griffith, 131
Edwards, Harry, 82–6, 96, 108–
  9, 111, 117, 125, 135, 136, 144,
  146–50, 156–8, 160–62, 164,
  166–74
Egyptians, ancient, 23, 24, 35, 38
Electricity, eighteenth-century
  curative applications of, 56
Elisha, 26, 31
Elizabeth I, 37
Elizabeth of Hungary, St, 34
Elliot, Rev. Maurice, 108
Ellman, E., 57
Ellwangen, Gassner's mass-meet-
  ings at, 44–5
Elves, intervention by, 33
Emmanuel movement, 104, 142,
  143
Empedocles, 25
England, Church of. See Church
  of England

Epidaurus, temples of, 24
Epilepsy, 33, 34, 37, 45
Episcopal church, of the USA, 104
Erysipelas, 34
Essenes, 27
Etheric vibrations, 85
Eustace, Father. See Lieshout, Hubert van
Evelyn, John, 42
Excreta, 33
Exorcism: in ancient times, 24; by Christ, 27, 90; regularized by Council of Antioch, 32; falls into disuse, 40; used by Gassner, 45; normal medieval panacea for mental ills, 88–9; in Church of England, 107
Extrasensory powers, 137
Eysenck, Professor, quoted, 17

Fabiola, 30
Fairies, intervention by, 33
Faith healing: objections to the term, 12–13; synonyms for, 13; scrupulous standards of examination required, 112; the evidence deserves serious attention, 113–14; nature of the sufferer and of the diseases treated, 114; the record more impressive with some types of disease than others, 114–15; three main outlooks, 116; comparison between Christian and Spiritualist results, 116–18; and psychological causes of illness, 119–23; and suggestion, 123–5, 127–8, 134; and mass emotionalism, 125; and role-playing, 125–7; and hypnotism, 128–32; and auto-suggestion, 132–4; and spontaneous remission, 134–5; question of permancy of cures, 135–6; and orthodox medical treatment, 135–7; evidence from the seventeenth century, 141; comparison of two groups of sufferers, with and without a paranormal element, 142–5; more critical investigations, 145–55; case histories, 156–64, 168–74; dying away of public interest in later 1950s, 166
Fatalism, 26, 31
Fatima, Portugal, healing shrine at, 92
Fellowship of St Luke, 104
Fiacre, St, 34
Fielding, Henry, 58
Fillan, St, 34
Fillmore, Charles and Myrtle, 62, 79
Fistula, 30, 42
Flamsteed, John, 42
Fox George, 97
France, spiritual healing in, 80
Frances Cabrini, St, 91
Francis of Assisi, St, 35
Francis Xavier, St, 35
Franklin, Benjamin, 55
Frayling, Margaret, 79
Free churches. See Dissenting sects
Freiburg, Institute of Psychology and Psychohygiene, 144
Freud, Sigmund, 119, 129
Fricker, Edward G., 76–7
Friends' Spiritual Healing Fellowship, 97
Fringe medicine, 13, 17
Functional diseases, 115

Galen, 25 72–3
Gallspach, castle, 57
Gandhi, M. K., 80
Garrett, Mrs Eileen J., 152
Gassner, Johann Joseph, 44–5, 52, 54, 59
Genovefa, St, 30
Germany, spiritual healing in, 80
Gibbon, Edward, 57–8
Gilbert, William, 55

Glastonbury, 33
Goitres, 76, 164
Goldney, Mrs K. M., 146
Gout, 37
Graham, Billy, 74
Graham, James, 57-8
Greatrakes, Valentine (the Stroker), 41-3, 45, 59, 73, 114
Greek Orthodox Church, 25, 93
Gregory Thaumaturgus, 30
Grensted, Canon L. W., 145-6
Guild of Health, 104
Guild of St Raphael, 104-5
Guillotin, Dr, 55

Haemorrhage, 27
Hall, Sir Edward Marshall, 71
Hall, Franklin, 75
Hamilton, Emma, Lady, 58
Harmonial philosophy, of Andrew Jackson Davis, 60
Hasidic movement, 58
Haydn, 53
Head diseases, 34
Healing beds, 58
Healing centres: medieval Christian shrines, 40; modern: Methodist, 76; non-denominational, 83, 102, 148; Roman Catholic, 91-6; Quaker, 97; Church of England, 103-4; Christian Science, 142
Healing orders, approved by Innocent III, 34
Healing saints. See under Saints
Healing sects, modern, 34
Healing temples, 25
Healing wells, 33
Health foods, 82. See also Herbs and herbalists
Hell, Father Maximilian, 52, 64
Helmont, Jan Baptista van, 39, 55, 115
Henry VIII, 38
Herbs and herbalists: in ancient medicine, 24, 30; medieval, 33, 34; modern, 77, 82, 85

Hermas, 30
Hickson, James Moore, 102-3, 104, 107
Hilarion, St, 30
Hofmans, Margaretha Greet, 80
Hohenlohe – Waldenburg – Schillingfürst, Prince von, 45-50, 63, 141
Holland, spiritual healing in, 80
Holmes, Rev. Alex, 97-8
Holywell, Flintshire, 33
Home, Daniel, 89
Home of Healing, Crowhurst, 103
Homoeopathy, 63, 77, 80, 82
Horder, Lord, 105, 167
Hungary, 50
Husband's Bosworth, 33
Hutchison, Rev. Harry, 98
Hutton, J. Bernard, 173
Huxford, A. T., 169
Hydropathic establishments, 33
Hydrophobia, 33
Hypnotism, 18, 56, 59, 61, 70, 71, 128-32, 178
Hysteria, 43, 53
Hysterical conversion, 122
Hysterical pregnancy, 126

Ignatius Loyola, St, 35
Imhotep, 24, 25, 72-3
Immunization, 13
Incantation, 24
Incubation temples, 25
Incurability, 134
India, healing saints in, 80
Infectious diseases, 114
Inglis, Brian, quoted, 137
Innocent III, Pope, 34
International Study Group on Unorthodox Healings, 153
Iona Community, 106
Irenaeus, 30
Iron, magical powers of, 55
Irvine, Dr R. E., 169, 171-2
Irvingites, 97
Italy, spiritual healing in, 80

Jacob, the Zouave, 50–52, 114
James I, 37
James, Henry, 60
Jeffrey, Very Rev. George Johnstone, 177
Jeffreys, Pastor, 96
Jesus of Nazareth, 27–8, 31, 43, 72, 88, 89, 101
Jewish Science movement, 67
Jews: Mosaic, 40; of later Rabbinical period, 32; modern, 87
John Bosco, St. See Bosco, St John
John, Father, of Kronstadt, 98
John the Baptist, 27
John of Beverley, 31
John, St, 29
Johnson, Dr Samuel, 38
Jones, R. F. McNab, 159
Judaic medicine, 26
Julian the Apostate, 30
Jung, Carl, 18; quoted, 88
Justinian, Emperor, 32
Justin Martyr, 30

Kappers, Dr, 153
Kardec, Allan, 70
Kat, Dr, 153
Kelly, G. A., 124
Kerin, Dorothy, 105
King's evil (scrofula), 37, 41
Kingsway Hall, London, meetings at, 111, 146
Kipling, Rudyard, quoted, 34
Knights Templar, 32
Knock, Ireland, healing shrine at, 92
Knowles, Frederick, 143
Koch, Robert, 56
Krishna, 26
Kyphoscoliosis, 160

Lambeth Committee (1920) on the Healing Ministry in the Christian Church, 107–8
Lameness, 37, 115
Lancet, 151
Lang, Andrew, 71

Lang, Archbishop Gordon, 108
La Salette, healing shrine at, 92
Lateran Council (1123), 32
Lavoisier, Antoine, 55
Lawrence, St, 34
Laying on of hands, 28, 29, 33, 36, 47, 61, 72, 97, 103, 106, 107, 117
Leech, 33
Lee penny, 33
Leprosy, 26, 37
Leuret, Dr François, 153
Liébeault, A. A., 129
Lie detector, 124
Lieshout, Hubert van (Father Eustace) 74
Light, Mary, 76
Lilley, William H., 77–9
Lister, Lord, 56, 84
Lloyd, Canon Roger, 108
Lodge, Sir Oliver, 71
London Healing Mission, 104
Loreto, healing shrine at, 92
Louis, St (Louis IX), 36
Louis XIV, 38, 141
Louis XVI, 54
Lourdes, 83, 93–6, 115, 117, 124, 150; Bureau des Constatations, 94, 149, 153
Loyola, St Ignatius. See Ignatius Loyola, St
Luther, Martin, 40, 97
Lyon, Margaret, 76

MacKenzie, Nan, 76
MacLeod, Lord, 106
Macmillan, William J., 79, 166
McPherson, Aimée Semple, 67, 97
MacRobert, Russell G., 149
Madge, H. A., 103
Madness, 34
Magic, 24, 39
Magic springs, 33
'Magnetic' healers. See d'Angelo, Achille; Ellman, E.; Mesmer, Friedrich Anton
Magnetism: Mesmer's theories

of animal magnetism, 54-5. 115; Mesmer's experiments, 55-6; eighteenth-century curative applications, 56

Mahommet, 32, 67, 154

Maillard, Rev. John, 103

Makhlouf, Charbel, 74

Malevolent spirits, 33

*Malleus Maleficarum*, 115

Mandus, Brother, 76

Marie Antoinette, 54

Martin, Pastor Bernard, 99-100

Martin of Tours, St, 31

Marvell, Andrew, 42

Mason, Dr A., 131

Massage, 77

Mass emotionalism, 125

Mass healings, 28, 29

Materialization of spirits, 69-70 (*and see* Spiritualism)

Materialist outlook, 116, 120

Mattingly, Mrs Anne, 49-50

May, Rev. Dr George, 98

Medical and Pastoral Service, Society for, 102

Medical practice, ancient and medieval : prediction and control of natural forces in earliest civilizations, 23; ancient middle-eastern cultures, 24; Greco-Roman, 24-5, 29-30, 35-6; ancient Far East, 26; Judaic, 26; Jesus of Nazareth, 27-8; the Apostles, 28-9; Fathers of the Church, 29-30; medieval Christian, 31-3; Jews of Rabbinical period, and Muslim, 32; folk medicine of western Europe, 32-4; intervention of saints, 34-5; royal healing, 35-8, 141; Reformation and Counter-Reformation, 39-40

Mediums, 70, 71, 72, 84, 85

Meningitis, 105

Mental illness, 28, 88; mentally-generated diseases (*see* Psychogenic diseases; Psychological

causes of illness)

Merlin, 33

Mesmer, Friedrich Anton, 52-7, 59, 62, 64, 115, 135, 141, 154

Metal-magic, 34

Methodism, 14, 96, 99-102; Society for Medical and Pastoral Service, 102

Michel, Martin, 46

Milton Abbey, Dorset, 103-4

Mind-body interaction, 19, 45, 130

Miracles, 27, 30, 116, 149-50; attitude of Roman Catholic Church, 89-92; Anglican attitude, 107

Monastery Hospitals, 32

Moon-magic, 33

Moral Rearmament, 97

Moravians, 97

Mormons, 97

Moses, 26

Mowatt, Dr Godfrey, 106

Mozart, 53

Multiple sclerosis, 135

Muscular diseases, 115

National Federation of Spiritual Healers, 169

Natural forces, prediction and control of, 23

Neolithic sites, 33

Neo-mesmerism, 57

Nephritis, 82 102

Neri, St Philip. *See* Philip Neri, St

New England, 60

New Life Healing Clinic, Baltimore, 76

New Life movement, 99

New Thought : Quimby's, 62; Miss McPherson's, 97

Newton, J. R., 60-61, 63

New York, 60, 61; Parapsychology Foundation Inc., 152, 166

Nicaea, Council of, 31

Nichols, Beverley, 11, 151

Nightingale, Florence, 60

Noel, Rev. Conrad, 104, 107

Nursing homes, Church of England, 105

Ockham's Razor, 112, 117
O'Connor, Barbara, 48
Ogilvie, Sir Heneage, quoted, 120
Okehampton, home of healing at, 104
Olaf, King of Iceland, 36
Oratorians, 35
Origen, 30; quoted, 118
Osborn, T. L., 75
Osler, Sir William, 123
Osteoarthritis, 163
Osteomyelitis, 76
Otilia, St, 34
Owen, Robert, 71

Palmistry, 17
Palsy, 43
Paracelsus, 39, 55, 115, 143
Paradies, Maria, 53
Paralysis, 53, 121, 157
Paranormal healing, as synonym for faith healing, 13 (and see Faith healing)
Parapsychology, 71; Parapsychology Foundation Inc., 152 166
Paré, Ambroise, 36
Pascal, 121
Pasteur, Louis, 84, 123
Paul, St, 29
Payne, Phoebe, 77-8
Pearce-Higgins, Canon J. D., 106
Peculiar People, the, 97
Peddie, Rev. J. Cameron, 98, 143
Peptic ulcers, 120
Pepys, Samuel, 38
Peregrine, St, 34
Perforated appendix, 82
Perkins, Elisha, 57
Persian medicine, 26
Peter, St, 28, 29
Philip, St, 29
Philip Neri, St, 35
Phrenology, 113, 128
Phthisis, 105

Pio, Padre, 74
Pistoia, healing beds of, 58
Placebos, 63, 123
Plagues, 114
Plato, 20, 39
Pliny, 43
Pneumatic therapy, 57
Poliomyelitis, 82
Pompeii, healing shine at, 92
Porta, Baptista, 55
'Positive thinking', 79
Post-mortem healing powers, of saints, 34
Poughkeepsie, 60
Poxes, 114
Prayer, 91, 122, 142
Presbyterians, 97-8
Prester John, 35
Prevision, 70
Priest-physicians of spiritual healing, 72
Priests: of early civilizations, 23, 24; early Christian, 29; alleged to have sold cures in medieval period, 32
Priory of St John, near Paris, 91
Prognosis, 23, 24, 77, 82
Protestantism: Calvinism, 40; dissenting sects, 96-102. See also Church of England; Scotland, Church of Pseudohypermuscular dystrophy, 164
Psyche, the, 121
Psychic News, 165; quoted, 161
Psychical Research, Society for, 70-71, 93, 146
Psychogenic diseases, 105, 119
Psychological causes of illness, 119-23
Psychosis, 40
Psychosomatic disease of the soul, 85-6
Pus of diseased cows, injection of, 56
Puységur, 56
Pyrrhus, King of Epirus, 35-6
Pythagorean number-magic, 39

Quadratus, 30
Quakers, 97, 116, 174
Quebec, healing shrine at, 92
Quimby, Phineas Parkhurst, 61–4
Quirinus, St, 34

Racanelli, Dr F., 80
Radiaesthesia, 17, 166
Raising the dead. See Resurrection of the dead
Rasputin, 80
Rayleigh, Lord, 71
Rectum, diseases of the, 34
Reformed churches, 98
Regensburg, Bishop of, 44
Rehder, Dr Hans, 144
Reichenbach, Baron von, 115
Relics of violent death, 33
Reptiles' dung, 33
Resurrection of the dead, 26, 79
Reversible actions, 122
Rheumatic disorders, 82, 98, 120, 163
Rhine, Dr, 149
Rhodes, Harriet, 79
Richards, Arthur, 77
Rings, blessing of, 37
Robert the Pious, 36
Robert of Shrewsbury, 11
Roberts, 'Reverend' Oral, 74
Roberts, Ursula, 76
Rochus, St, 34
Rogers, George, 167
Role-playing, 125–7
Roman Catholic church, 14, 24, 74, 75, 105, 174; and incubation cures, 25; healing saints, 30–31, 32; formalization of doctrine, 31; monastery hospitals, 32; abuses by priesthood, 32; and royal healing, 37; healing shrines, 40; and communion of saints, 69–70; investigations of lives of spiritual healers, 74; outlook on paranormal healing, 87–8; and sickness as God's will, 88; and exorcism, 88–9;

and miracles, 89–92; modern healing saints, 91; and healing powers of those outside the faith, 91–2; and Lourdes, 93–6
Rosenthal, 126
Rosicrucians, 72
Royal East Sussex Hospital, 169
Royal Festival Hall, London, 148
Royal healing, 35–8, 141
Russia, 19–20, 80
Ryle, Professor, 20

St Albans, 32
St Bartholomew's Hospital, 159
Saints: healing saints, 30–31, 32, 91; spiritual cures worked by intervention of, 34–5; communion of, 69–70
Salerno, 40
Salmon, Mrs Elsie (the 'Lady in White'), 75–6
Sanford, Mrs Agnes, 75
Sargant, Dr William, Battle for the Mind, 119, 179
Scandinavia, spiritual healing in, 80
Scherzer, Carl, 141
Schlatter, Francis, 62
Schwartzenberg, Mathilde von, 46
Science and Health (Mary Baker Eddy), 64, 67, 68
Scotland (Presbyterian) Church of, 106
Scrofula. See King's evil
Searle, George, 105
'Seekers', 72
Self-induced hypnosis, 78, 132, 134
Semantics, 124
Sensory deprivation, 127
Serapis, 25
Servadio, Professor, 138
Seventh sons of seventh sons, occult powers attributed to, 33
Sevigné, Mme de, 39
Sexual anxiety, 58
Shakespeare, 37

Sharp, Ven. A. F., 106
Shere, Surrey, Harry Edward's sanctuary at, 83, 148
Short, Dr Rendle, quoted, 117
Shortness of breath, 43
Signs and omens, 82
Sikora, Madame, 74
Silent Unity fellowship of the Fillmores, 62
Simpson, C. A., 76
Slipped disc, 159–60
Smith, Joseph, 97
Smith, Millicent, 79
Snake-bite, 26, 29, 100
Snake-worship, 75
Solomon, 26
Somervell, Dr Howard, 93
Soper, Lord, 99
Soubirous, Bernadette. See Bernadette, St
Soul, the, 121–2; psychosomatic disease of, 85–6
South Africa, 79
Southern California, 60
Spiritualism, 69–71, 85, 95–6, 100, 101, 106, 116, 117, 125, 145, 150, 178
Spiritual maladies, question of their existence, 121–2
Spondylosis, 161, 168–72
Spontaneous remission, 134–5
Springs, magic, 33
Stanford, E. W., 80
Stead, W. T., 71
Steiner, Rudolf, 62
Stephen, St, 29
Stigmata, 98, 121
Stones, alleged prevention of hydrophobia by, 33–4
Strauch, Dr Inge, 144
Stroker, the. See Greatrakes, Valentine
Stroking, 37, 47
Suggestion, 119, 123–5, 127–8, 133–4
Sundar Singh, Sadhu, 80
Sun worship, 75

Supernatural phenomena, 70
Superstition, 87
Surgery, 13, 24, 33, 34
Svengali, 56
Sweating, 33
Swedenborg, 62, 149
Switzerland, spiritual healing in, 80
Symonds, J. A., 71
Sympathetic healing, 39
Sympathetic rites, 24
Synchronized private prayer, 48
Syndrome shift, 120–21

Taliesin, 33
Talismans, 33
Tarpey, Mrs Kingsley, 76
Tatian, 30
Teeth diseases, 34
Telegnosis, 18
Telepathy, 70, 137
Temple, Archbishop William, 108
Tennyson, Lord, 71
Tertullian, 30
Therapy, original meaning of the term, 28
Theresa of Avila, St, 35
Thomas à Becket, St. See Becket
Thought microbes, 62
Thouless, Dr, 147–8; quoted, 144, 146–7
Throat diseases, 34, 91
Thurston, Father Herbert, 41; quoted, 66, 116–17
Toes, laying on of, 35–6
Toothache, 28
Touch, healing by, 35–6, 76
Trampler, Dr Kurt, 144
Trance, 45, 52–3; mesmerically-induced, 55, 56
Trauma healing, 114
Trent, Council of, 105
Tribal sovereign, healing by, 35
Trudel, Dorothy, 98
Tuberculosis, 119, 142
Tuberculous peritonitis, 105
Turner, Gordon, 76

Twain, Mark, 65, 174

Ulcers, 37, 120
Unction, 32, 105, 107
Unitarians, 97
Urban, Professor, 153
Utrecht conference, 152–4

Vasomotor rhinitis, 159
Vespasian, Emperor, 36, 43
Vianney, St John (the Curé d'Ars), 91
Vincent Ferrer, St, 35
Virgin Mary, 92
Vitus, St, 34

Wainwright House, New York, 80
Waldenses, 97
Wales, 33–4
Ward, Joshua ('Spot'), 58
Warlocks, 33
Weatherhead, Dr Leslie, 99–102, 105, 108, 122, 132, 166
Webber, Jack, 85
Wells, healing, 33
Wesley, John, 99
West, Dr D. J., 94–6, 120
White Ladies, healing sect of, 33
White witchcraft, 34
Wickland, Carl, 40

Wilbur, Sybil, 141
William III, 38
William of Malmesbury, 36
Wilson, Rev. James, 104
Winefride, St, 11, 33, 94
Wise woman, 33
Witchcraft, 61; white, 34
Witch doctors, 23
Witches, 33
Withered limbs, 76
Wizards, healing, 25, 33
Woodard, Dr Christopher, 81–2, 86, 108, 150–51, 173
Woods, Rev. Bertram, 20, 100, 102, 115–16, 146
Worrall, Ambrose and Olga, 79
Wyatt, Thomas, 75
Wyman, Rev. F. L., 117

Xavier, St Francis. See Francis Xavier, St
'X-ray sight', 77

Yoga, 26, 131
York, Archbishop of, 108

Zeileis, Valentin, 57
Zion City, 79–80
Zola, Émile, 93
Zouave, the. See Jacob
Zweig, Stefan, quoted, 67